CHAMPS2

Realising
Transformational
Change

London: TSO

Published by TSO (The Stationery Office)
and available from:
Online
www.tsoshop.co.uk

Mail, Telephone, Fax & E-mail
TSO
PO Box 29, Norwich, NR3 1GN
Telephone orders/General enquiries:
0870 600 5522
Fax orders: 0870 600 5533
E-mail: customer.services@tso.co.uk
Textphone: 0870 240 3701

TSO@Blackwell and other Accredited Agents

Customers can also order publications from:
TSO Ireland
16 Arthur Street, Belfast BT1 4GD
Tel 028 9023 8451 Fax 028 9023 5401

CHAMPS2®

APMG-International
Sword House
Totteridge Road
High Wycombe
HP13 6DG
Contact: servicedesk@apmgroup.co.uk
Web: www.apmg-international.com
www.champs2.info

First edition 2010

ISBN 9780117068674

CONTENTS

List of Figures and Tables

Foreword

Glyn Evans is the originator of CHAMPS2, which has led to many successful transformational change programmes.

'The need to change the way our organisations operate has probably never been greater. Often, incremental change is insufficient and it is necessary to fundamentally rethink and radically redesign what a business or organisation does in order that it can flourish in a changing world. Major transformational change is a complex process, requiring clear direction, excellent planning, specialist resources and, above all, a massive commitment from your organisation. Achieving all this is not simple.

'The delivery of transformational change has the development of a new vision for future service delivery at its heart. This has then to be supported by proven approaches to the holistic redesign of services, addressing each component – process, people and technology – and their implementation. Most importantly, there needs to be a focus on making sure that the promised benefits are realised.

'The CHAMPS2 method will help you to define that clear vision for the organisation and then provide you with a method or pathway that will help you to realise the vision and measurable Benefits.

'CHAMPS2 asks, 'If you were creating this service now, what outcomes would you be looking to deliver? What measures will you use to be able to know you've achieved those outcomes? How would you design your service to realise those outcomes?' This method therefore fundamentally reviews all aspects of the service delivery area involved and concentrates on the realisation of outcomes, not primarily on process.

'This manual will provide you with the tools you need to transform your organisation.'

Glyn Evans
Corporate Director of Business Change
Birmingham City Council

Acknowledgements

Authoring team
Elena Martin
Sheena Atkinson
Sarah Hinksman
Morten Bonde

CHAMPS2 reference group

Kate Blackall	I-Logic
Sue Childs	PRINCE2 Examiner
Nick Denington	HCL AXON
Martyn Hedges	SCOLL Methods Ltd
Piotr Kotelnicki	CRM Poland
Leah Radstone	APMG
Chris Tanner	Afiniti
David Watson	ADt Partnership

Contributors

Paul Bayliss	Service Birmingham
Trung Bui	Capita
Brian Ellis	Service Birmingham
Mumtaz Mohammed	Service Birmingham
Gill Terry	Birmingham City Council

The authors would also like to thank
APMG
Birmingham City Council
Service Birmingham

We are very grateful for the contribution of the CHAMPS2 Foundation and Practitioner pilot groups which took place in Birmingham 2008-2010.

THE ORIGINS OF CHAMPS2

CHAMPS2 was originally developed to satisfy a requirement to manage transformational change within Birmingham City Council. The requirement arose out of the complexity of the changes to process, organisational and technology that were initiated in the city.

Birmingham City Council (BCC) is one of the largest councils in the UK. Back in 2003, BCC was in many ways far from being at the leading edge of local government. It was clear that an unprecedented scale of change would be required.

From the start, the programme in Birmingham was intended to deliver radical, large-scale change. It was not just concerned with the modernisation of information systems. To be truly transformational, meant making radical alternations to processes, organisational structures, job roles and accountabilities, and cultures.

The journey towards transformation would affect the entire council's operation, service delivery, personnel, and the citizens of Birmingham.

DEVELOPMENT OF CHAMPS2

A single approach to business transformation was required that would provide consistency, using a common language and tools and reproducing best practice and templates. It was essential that this focussed on service redesign.

The common approach provided programme teams with a best practice Vision led, Benefits driven method, tools and templates, complemented by a Quality Management Framework. This became known as CHAMPS2, an abbreviation of 'change management in the public sector'. As the method developed, it was made generic and suitable for use in private, public and voluntary sectors.

MAKING RADICAL TRANSFORMATION HAPPEN

CHAMPS2 manages the risks of radical transformation through three key elements:

- **The development of business cases**
  Business cases are developed systematically through the early phases of CHAMPS2. The Full Business Case is comprehensive, detailing the outcomes to be achieved, the cost and Benefits of implementing the new ways of working and, importantly, the evidence base to support the argument for investment.

- **The definition and ownership of Benefits**
  All identified outcomes will result in the production of one or more Benefit Cards. Each Benefit Card has a Benefit Owner who is responsible and accountable for the realisation of that Benefit.

■ *An emphasis on Benefits realisation*

CHAMPS2 emphasises throughout, the importance of realising defined Benefits and there is a particular focus on this towards the end of the journey. All Benefits are recorded, and their realisation monitored, centrally. There is, therefore, an early warning system in place if Benefits delivery starts to go off-track, allowing appropriate corrective action to be carried out.

In summary, CHAMPS2 is intended to embed good practice in transformational change management and leadership.

OBJECTIVES OF THE MANUAL

This manual is designed as a reference tool for those working in transformation teams and as a guide to CHAMPS2 for those studying for the Foundation and Practitioner examinations.

After studying this manual you will be able to:
■ Understand CHAMPS2 components: phases, stages and activities
■ Explain the principles underpinning CHAMPS2
■ Understand the purpose and composition of CHAMPS2 products
■ Explain the rationale behind the CHAMPS2 processes
■ Identify relationships between CHAMPS2 processes and products
■ Apply CHAMPS2 within the context of your own working environment
■ Tailor CHAMPS2 to meet differing programme requirements and challenges.

STRUCTURE OF THE MANUAL

Section I provides an introduction to CHAMPS2 and to finding your way around the manual.

Section II is a detailed guide to the full CHAMPS2 method, covering every phase, stage and activity.

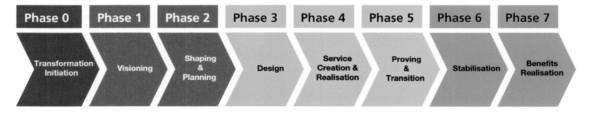

Section III covers the CHAMPS2 themes as follows:
■ Quality Management Framework
■ Governance
■ Benefits management.

Appendices
Appendix 1 CHAMPS2 core products
Appendix 2 Phase Exit Criteria Checklists
Appendix 3 CHAMPS2 Glossary

Section I
Introduction to CHAMPS2

SECTION I – INTRODUCTION TO CHAMPS2

OBJECTIVES OF THIS SECTION

This section is in three chapters and will introduce you to CHAMPS2 and help you to understand:

- *How CHAMPS2 supports delivery of transformational change*
- *How to find your way around the manual*
- *The key principles of applying CHAMPS2 in your organisation.*

Chapter 1 – CHAMPS2 Overview

CHAMPS2 supports the effective delivery of transformational change. It minimises the risk of transformational change programmes by following an organised route in the form of a tried and tested set of steps organised into phases.

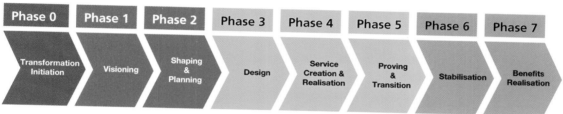

Figure I.1 – Phases of CHAMPS2

CHAMPS2 provides:

- A detailed, structured, but flexible pathway
- Opportunities to tailor the path for individual change programmes
- A consistent approach and language that can be used across change initiatives.

BENEFITS OF CHAMPS2

CHAMPS2 is designed to deliver radical change, whatever the size of organisation and can be used alongside established project and programme management methods. In brief it:

▪ Focuses on realising business Benefits

It is a Vision-led, Benefits-driven approach. This means that it focuses on a big picture Vision developed to unite the organisation behind change. It is structured to deliver tangible Benefits to customers, the organisation and staff, and uses communication, stakeholder management and change management approaches to make sure that everyone involved understands what difference the transformational change will make.

▪ Supports the end-to-end transformational journey

CHAMPS2 covers the whole transformational change journey, from the initial definition of strategic need and strategic Outcomes, through to Benefits realisation.

▪ Is flexible

It is a method which can be easily tailored to projects and programmes of different scales, or brought in to use at different points in their lifecycles.

CHAMPS2 can be used on both full-scale radical change programmes and smaller change initiatives.

■ **Incorporates practical tools and techniques**
CHAMPS2 provides a route map through the complex process of transformational change with detailed activity descriptions and resources. It is rich in content, offering practical help to complement this manual in the form of templates, examples and 'how to' documents, which can be found on the CHAMPS2 Knowledge Centre at **www.champs2.info**. This allows programmes to concentrate on making the transformational change happen within the framework provided.

ABOUT TRANSFORMATIONAL CHANGE

Transformational change
Radical change to create better products and services whilst using resources more efficiently.

CHAMPS2 is a method that is led by a Vision for the organisation. It is driven by tangible business Benefits that need to be achieved in order to make any change sustainable. Using CHAMPS2 will enable the organisation to clearly define the Vision and realise the business Benefits. It addresses three principal areas for change in the business – processes, organisation structure and technology.

It should be stressed from the outset that transformational change is not an objective in its own right; its purpose is to help deliver the improvements and Benefits that the business seeks for:
■ Customers – better services and products
■ Employees – greater job satisfaction
■ Efficiency – better use of resources, doing more for less money.

And, in turn, this rewards stakeholders – for example, by offering greater return on investment.

The support and commitment of leaders within the organisation to the change play an especially crucial role in the success of the transformation journey. Leaders need to be prepared to spearhead the transformational change to deliver the corporate Vision for the future.

HOW CHAMPS2 WORKS
Phases, stages and activities
CHAMPS2 divides transformational change into eight phases, which are illustrated below. These phases guide us from the beginning (the strategic need) to the end (the strategic Outcome). They are colour coded to reflect the movement towards green Benefits realisation. The phases are introduced in more detail later in this chapter.

The eight phases are broken down into stages, each one of which will achieve a specific objective; for example, determining strategic needs.

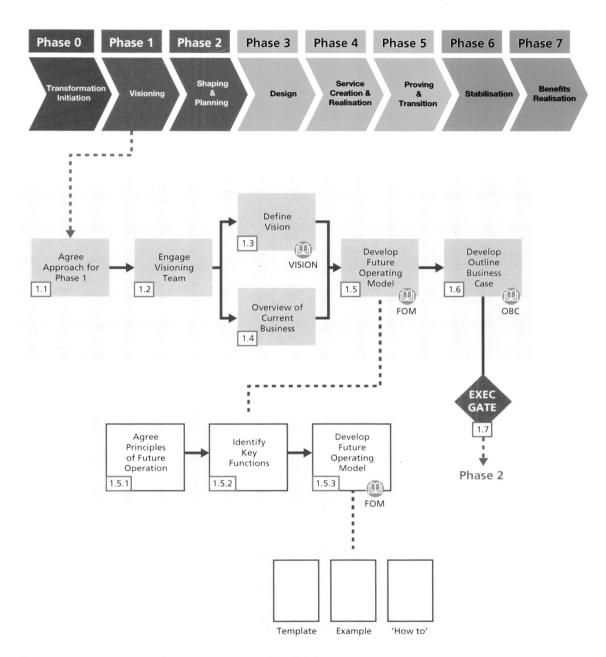

Figure I.2 – CHAMPS2 phases, stages and activities

Within the stages are a varying number of activities that can be followed to complete the stage. For example, as part of selecting a new IT system, the selection criteria need to be set and potential systems need to be identified.

Each phase, stage and activity has a number, for example, activity 2.11.8. The first number indicates the phase number, such as phase 2 – Shaping and Planning. The second number indicates the stage within that phase, such as stage 2.11 – Develop programme governance. The final number belongs to the activity. In this example, 2.11.8 is the activity Develop training strategy.

CHAMPS2 products

The output from stages and activities are products; some of these are physical documents, such as a Full Business Case; and some of them are events, such as obtaining approval.

Essential documents within CHAMPS2 are called 'core products'. There are three types of core products:

- Quality management products help to assure quality and adherence to CHAMPS2, and provide exit criteria at the end of each phase.
- Milestone products are those which, when approved, allow the programme to continue to the next stage or phase. They provide control over the transformation journey.
- Transformation products support the evolution of the new processes, organisation and technology, and their successful delivery.

CHAMPS2 gates

Control gates are a feature of CHAMPS2 that will ensure that risks are minimised and budgets or funding released. They are points during transformational change where products and progress are checked and approved. The OGC Gateway Process examines programmes and projects at key decision points in their lifecycle. It looks ahead to provide assurance that they can progress successfully to the next stage.

There are two types of gate in CHAMPS2:

- The Executive gates are concerned with investment decisions at the beginning of the journey and return on investment or Benefits at the end
- The Programme Board gates are concerned with checking progress and are used predominantly during programme delivery.

There is more information about CHAMPS2 roles, gates and governance in section III.

THE PHASES OF THE CHAMPS2 LIFECYCLE

The table below introduces each phase and some of the core products which
will be produced.

Phase 0 – Transformation Initiation
In this phase, leaders of the organisation:

- Determine the strategic need for transformation
- Formulate the strategic Outcomes
- Determine the strategic Benefits.

Indicative costs of transformation are determined and funding options considered.
The information is documented within the Strategic Business Case.

Phase 1 – Visioning
Here, the potential operation of the business in the future is explored. It will be described
in the:

- Vision – comprising Vision statement and Outcomes
- Future Operating Model – outlining the composition and operation of
  the changed organisation.

An Outline Business Case is produced at the end of this phase, which will set out
the transformation required and will form the basis for the development of the Full
Business Case.

Phase 2 – Shaping and Planning
Whilst the previous phases identified the need for transformational change, this phase
defines the programme that will achieve it.
The phase consists of:

- Scoping and shaping ('the what') – defining the scope and objectives
  of the programme, and outlining the solution in the form of a Logical
  Design
- Structuring the programme ('the how') – defining the programme
  structure and governance and developing high-level plans in order to
  estimate costs and timescales.

A Full Business Case is produced at the end of this phase, providing a detailed justification
for transformational change based on measurable Benefits.

Phase 3 – Design

This phase develops the detailed design of the solution that will achieve the desired Outcomes and deliver the promised Benefits.

The three stages of design add a more detailed level of understanding and show how processes, the organisation structure and technology fit together.

- The detailed design builds on the scope and processes identified within the Logical Design and defines how the service will operate and what changes are required in the business
- The Full Business Case is checked to ensure that it is still valid now that more is known about the solution and how it will be delivered
- The Functional Specifications define in detail how the new solution will operate.

Phase 4 – Service Creation and Realisation

During this phase, the detailed design will be converted into a tangible solution:

- A new organisation for the business that will support the newly designed ways of working
- New and updated process documents, such as policies, standards and procedures, will be written or updated to support the new ways of working
- New technology components will be created or configured and fully tested.

The last element of this phase is end-to-end testing of business processes to ensure that the solution is fit for purpose before being passed over to the business areas.

Phase 5 – Proving and Transition

This phase contains three main areas of work:

- Further testing of the solution in the form of user acceptance testing (UAT) and operational acceptance testing (OAT), to prove that the solution will work in real business situations and that it is robust, with suitable support processes in place.
- Transitional activities to prepare the business and technology for going live, such as populating the new organisation structure, training, setting up infrastructure or hardware and software installations.
- Going live – actually switching to the new ways of working.

Phase 6 – Stabilisation

Phase 6 seeks to:

- Stabilise the solution and optimise all elements of its performance
- Ensure the solution is fully adopted by the business
- Realise early Benefits.

Phase 7 – Benefits Realisation

This is the final phase, which ensures that the Benefits of transformational change are actually achieved and are sustainable. It includes two main areas of work:

- Measuring and evaluating Benefits
- Making improvements to the solution and ensuring that these are in line with the overall Vision and that they support Benefits realisation.

Chapter 2 – Using the manual

AIMS OF THE MANUAL

This manual is designed to:

- Provide an insight into the detail of CHAMPS2 and its principles, as well as the purpose and the sequence of stages
- Cover the syllabus of the CHAMPS2 Foundation and Practitioner examinations
- Illustrate the themes that go across CHAMPS2.

www.champs2.info

CHAMPS2 is also available as an online resource at www.champs2.info.

The online version of CHAMPS2 offers more detail and additional resources including templates for core products, 'how to' guides and examples from other organisations. Although it is possible to use CHAMPS2 without the additional material, accessing it will save time and effort.

There is also a user community on **www.champs2.info** to facilitate communications between people using CHAMPS2 and to share best practice and experiences.

STRUCTURE OF THE MANUAL

The manual is divided into three main sections:

- Section I – CHAMPS2 introduction
- Section II – CHAMPS2 process: This provides a detailed view of the stages and activities which make up the phases.
- Section III – CHAMPS2 themes:
  - ☐ Quality management
  - ☐ Governance
  - ☐ Benefits management

The appendix includes descriptions of all CHAMPS2 core products, Phase Exit Criteria Checklists and a glossary.

HOW CAN THE CHAMPS2 MANUAL HELP YOU?

Different people will use the manual in different ways, and it will probably depend on why you want to get to know more about CHAMPS2, what your role is, and whether you are thinking about, or are involved in, a transformation programme. Plan to read the whole manual to understand the process in detail, but if you are using it to help you in a particular role, look at the table below to see what support the CHAMPS2 manual can provide.

Leader/Executive	As a leader, you may be asking, 'What change is required?', 'What are our ambitions?', 'How ready is the business for change?', 'What is the business doing right now that we want to change?'. You should: Read the purpose/overview sections for each of the phases in section II Consider reading this section and phases 0 and 1 in detail Read the chapters on Benefits management and the Quality Management Framework in section III Use the diagrams in the remaining phases to see where the method will take you.
Senior manager/ change manager	As a senior manager you have vision for what the business could achieve. Your questions may focus on looking at this situation in a completely different way. For example: 'Could we depart from the habits that have held us back?'. It may be that there are external pressures for change – such as legislation, responsibilities to stakeholders or the need to make budget changes. Sometimes continuous improvement and business as usual is not enough. To get started: ■ Consider reading the whole manual in detail because you will need a full understanding of the method ■ Explore the themes with a particular focus on Benefits management.
Business manager	As a business manager you need to consider your particular requirements and where your area sits in a potential transformational change programme. To get started: Review the phases in section II of the manual Identify any of the phases that are of immediate relevance to you and your area Explore the themes and, in particular, Benefits management, to familiarise yourself with the range of things that could apply in your area.
Human resources or people development specialist	To get started: ■ Review the phases in section II of the manual to get a feel for the coverage ■ Explore the themes and, in particular, organisation design, to familiarise yourself with how the method addresses changes to the organisation structure.
Design authority	You are likely to be particularly interested in redesigning processes, the organisation structure and/or technology, because you know there are improvements that could help the organisation to work more efficiently. To get started: Consider reading and understanding phases 3 and 4 in detail Explore the themes and, in particular, the process, organisation and technology design themes Flick through the remainder of section II of the manual to get a feel for the coverage.

Programme/ Project Manager	You need some detail. Don't lose sight of your project management skills and tools: you will continue to need them. To fully understand how CHAMPS2 can support you: ☐ Consider reading the whole manual in detail; you will need a full understanding of the method and all of the themes ☐ Identify any of the phases that are of immediate relevance to you and your area ☐ Explore the themes, with particular focus on CHAMPS2 governance, to familiarise yourself with the range of things that could apply in your area.
Candidate for accreditation	You will need a detailed knowledge and understanding of the CHAMPS2 method. Read the whole manual in detail because you will need a full understanding of the method and all of the themes.

Table I.1 – How different people might use the manual

Chapter 3 – Applying CHAMPS2 in your organisation

CHAMPS2 is designed to review all aspects of service delivery within a business area. It not only provides a structured approach to delivering change, but it can also be adapted for use in a range of scenarios and for change initiatives of different magnitudes.

This chapter explains how CHAMPS2 can be tailored to the size and type of programme. It introduces the Quality Management Framework, which is used throughout the change journey to assure quality. In this context it can also help to select the parts of CHAMPS2 that are the most appropriate to use for each change initiative.

SCALING CHAMPS2

CHAMPS2 can be applied in a range of situations and should be used in the way that suits the particular initiative. It may not be necessary to use all eight phases of CHAMPS2. For example:

- **Transformational change programme**
  Where the size and scope of change is significant, the programme should adopt all eight phases of CHAMPS2. A pathway through the stages and activities that meet the needs and Outcomes of the business should be defined using the Phase Quality Plan in the Quality Management Framework (explored in more detail in section III of this manual).

- **Programme already in progress**
  Organisations may be using CHAMPS2 to finish a partially completed change initiative or a programme that has gone adrift. For example, CHAMPS2 could be used from phase 3 onwards. The Phase Exit Criteria Checklist is the tool used to check that the groundwork has been carried out and all the information required in phase 3, such as the Vision and Future Operating Model, is in place.

- **Smaller or non-transformational programmes or projects**
  Other business areas may be embarking on a new programme of change with a narrower scope or where the impact will not be widespread. These organisations should define a pathway through phases 0 to 2 to get a clear picture of what is required and then pay particular attention to structuring a change programme that meets their needs.

- **Proof of concept projects**
  There are projects that do not necessarily proceed to live implementation, such as proof of concept. These projects could start from phase 3 – Design and finish with testing as outlined in phase 4 – Service Creation and Realisation. When a proof of concept is required to complete the design it may be more efficient to incorporate activities from another phase into the current phase rather than create a separate project.

CHAMPS2 can also be applied as a tool box to complement existing methodologies within the organisation, using the product descriptions in this manual and the associated templates and examples, available from the Knowledge Centre at **www.champs2.info**.

APPLYING CHAMPS2 TO DIFFERENT PROGRAMME STRUCTURES

The scope which is developed in phase 2 – Shaping and Planning should provide a clear idea of which business areas and services are being transformed, which customer groups are affected and which capabilities need to be delivered. In most cases it will be unmanageable to deliver it all as one project.

Here are some examples of how the programme can be structured based on different perspectives:

- **Benefits**
  By taking a Benefits driven approach we will be looking at what needs to be delivered to achieve a particular Benefit or a set of Benefits. This is likely to deliver Benefits effectively, but may not be the most cost-effective approach.

- **Service or product**
  Programmes could be defined based on groups of services or products, for example, implementing a document management system across the whole business, before any other changes are put in place. This may be a cost-effective approach, but may not lead to early Benefits realisation.

- **Customer group**
  Programmes could be structured so that all the services aimed at a particular customer group are delivered together. These groups may be where the most work is required or where the Benefits are highest. Because all aspects of the solution will need to be provided for each customer group separately, this may not be the most cost-effective option.

- **Location**
  Programme delivery could be split by priority geographical areas. Again, it may mean that greater Benefits are delivered in those locations where quick results can be achieved. The disadvantage could be that the timeframe for delivering in every area is extended, and coverage, using the new solution, could be patchy and inconsistent.

- **Quick wins**
  Priority areas of the business could be those where there is the potential to realise Benefits quickly. In particular, financial savings, which may provide funding for further transformation. This can be a tempting approach, but care needs to be taken to ensure that the customer focus is not lost.

Once the approach is agreed, and the programme is structured into work streams and projects, CHAMPS2 will branch accordingly. The diagram below illustrates how CHAMPS2 can be applied to a typical programme structure. There is likely to be only one stream of work for phases 0 to 2 and from then on there may be several work streams or projects going through CHAMPS2 at their own pace.

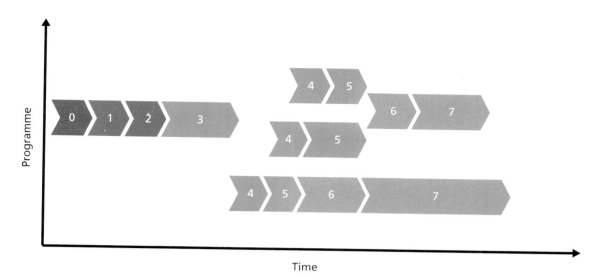

Figure I.3 – Applying CHAMPS2 to different programme work streams

Projects within a programme need to be co-ordinated to take account of instances where one project is dependent on another. The length of each phase may vary, and phase 7 – Benefits Realisation, may take considerably longer than some of the other phases to complete. It is vital that each stage of each phase is completed to an appropriate and agreed level, as each will have an impact on those that follow.

Whilst the CHAMPS2 method can provide guidance on the sequence of products and activities that will achieve successful business change, the actual delivery needs to be managed by standard programme and project management methods such as PRINCE2® and MSP®.

DETAILED TAILORING OF CHAMPS2
Once the high-level approach has been determined, i.e. the phases that will be used, and the programme structure, CHAMPS2 can be tailored within each phase. Each phase starts by using the Quality Management Framework to determine the approach that the particular programme wants to take, including the products that will need to be delivered. For example, an organisation might already have an excellent training strategy in place which can be used rather than developing a new one. It makes sense to use existing good practice where appropriate and to use CHAMPS2 alongside existing strategies and methods that work well in your organisation. An active decision is taken about what is appropriate to include in the programme and what may be left out.

These choices are documented at the start of each phase in a:
- Phase Quality Plan which describes how CHAMPS2 will be tailored to the individual programme. It is a tool that can be used to review each of the stages and activities and decide, backed up by reasons, which ones should be undertaken and, consequently, which products will be produced.
- Product Quality Plan which defines the products in detail and how they will be produced, reviewed and approved.

Whilst tailoring it is important to review the Phase Exit Criteria Checklist to ensure that the objectives of each phase are met.

Descriptions of the Phase Quality Plan, the Product Quality Plan and the Phase Exit Criteria Checklist can be found in section III and in appendix 1. The criteria contained in all the Phase Exit Criteria Checklists are also listed in appendix 2.

Section II
CHAMPS2 Process

SECTION II – CHAMPS2 PROCESS

CHAMPS2 is made up of eight phases which move from strategic needs to the strategic Outcomes and deliver Benefits for the business.

This section will take you through CHAMPS2, exploring the stages that make up each phase, core products and roles and responsibilities.

OBJECTIVES OF THIS SECTION
After reading this section you will understand:
- *The complete transformational change journey*
- *How each phase and stage builds on the previous one and contributes to the next*
- *How Benefits are managed through the phases*
- *The importance of a holistic view of change which includes processes, organisation structure and technology.*

How section II works
Each of the eight phases starts with an overview of the purpose of the phase and roles and responsibilities. There is a diagram showing the phase within CHAMPS2 and the stages that make up the phase. You can then go through the detail of the stages and activities to understand how it works.

NUMBERING
Phases are numbered 0 to 7. Stages are then numbered 0.1, 0.2 within phase 0, and so on. Activities are then numbered sequentially within the stage. For example, activity 2.7.3 would be the third activity in the seventh stage within phase 2.

DIAGRAMS
Diagrams throughout the manual illustrate the sequencing of activities associated with each stage. These numbered diagrams are also reproduced in the online CHAMPS2 Knowledge Centre, where they are accompanied by activity descriptions and other material.

To help guide you through the process some underlying themes which are fundamental to the CHAMPS2 process are highlighted with blocks of colour in the stage diagrams and corresponding colours in the activity descriptions.

Benefits	Process	Organisation	Technology

Gates are represented on the diagrams by a diamond shape:

Products are represented by a document icon:

Phase 0 – Transformation Initiation

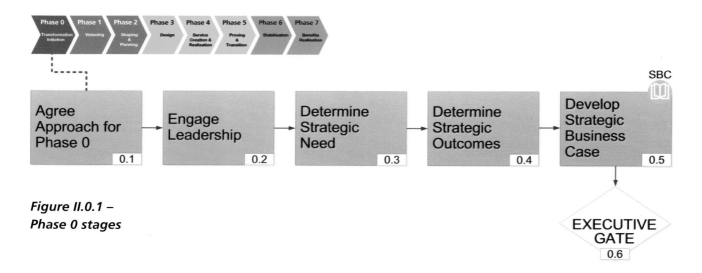

Figure II.0.1 –
Phase 0 stages

Phase 0
Explores the strategic need for change and identifies leaders' aspirations in the form of strategic Outcomes. It is also the phase during which the Strategic Business Case is created and budgetary funding is secured.

PURPOSE OF PHASE 0 – TRANSFORMATION INITIATION

Phase 0 is designed to help to make the decision about whether transformation is required. If so, leaders need to make a 'space' for the new transformation initiative. It entails identifying where the business as a whole wants to be and developing the Strategic Business Case.

It is important for leaders to be engaged from the outset and a Senior Responsible Owner should be appointed within this phase. Leaders will consider the strategic need for change, the ultimate goals for the customer and the organisation, and earmark the money required to carry out transformation.

ROLES AND RESPONSIBILITIES

Executive – People within the business who decide whether to make the investment in transformational change. This could be an existing group and is typically at executive level.

Leadership – This group is responsible for moving the transformational change agenda forwards and championing it throughout the journey.

Senior Responsible Owner – A person within the business who provides direction and focus and who contributes to investment decisions on behalf of the Executive.

Phase 0 team – A small team which facilitates leadership engagement and development of the Strategic Business Case.

Quality Assurance Function – This group provides advice and monitors progress in terms both of quality and the use of CHAMPS2.

0.1 AGREE APPROACH FOR PHASE 0

Purpose

CHAMPS2 can be tailored to each individual programme. This stage sets the agenda for the phase and ensures that the path through the method and the approach to deliver the required products are agreed.

Stage 0.1 consists of the following activities:

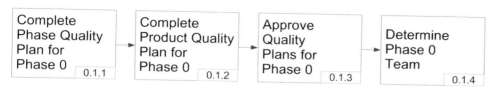

Figure II.0.2 – Activities in stage 0.1 – Agree approach for phase 0

0.1.1 – 0.1.3 Quality Plans

The approach for phase 0 – Transformation Initiation will be captured in two documents that are central to maintaining quality standards and managing client expectations:

- **Phase Quality Plan** – to tailor the stages and activities to the programme's needs
- **Product Quality Plan** – to ensure the quality of each product and how it is approved.

At the end of the phase, the **Phase 0 Exit Criteria Checklist** should be used to assess whether the phase objectives have been met. This document, therefore, forms a vital input into the development of Quality Plans and should be considered when they are being created.

The Phase Quality Plan and the Product Quality Plan are not formally agreed until they have been approved. Both documents have to be approved by the:
- Senior Responsible Owner
- Phase 0 team leader
- Quality Assurance Function.

Key products from the Quality Management Framework are fully explained in section III of this manual.

0.1.4 Determine phase 0 team

Phase 0 is about exploring potential areas for change and setting the strategic Outcomes. It is typically initiated by the Senior Responsible Owner of the change programme. A small team is required to facilitate leadership engagement and challenge the status quo. They should stimulate transformational thinking and develop the Strategic Business Case. The team could consist of a transformational change expert, business change managers and subject matter experts.

This is often an appropriate point at which to begin considering what level and type of communication and consultation will be helpful during this phase, in preparation for the activity in stage 0.6.

0.2 ENGAGE LEADERSHIP

Purpose

Who will lead?

Stakeholders and a leadership team are critical, and the process of engaging with the right people in the right way can make a big difference to the success of any transformational change programme.

Getting buy-in at the highest level should be a planned and managed process. The Senior Responsible Owner, or the Sponsor who is the originator of the transformational change idea, should have initial discussions with leaders of the organisation about the potential for transformation.

Once leaders are fully engaged, the transformation potential can be further explored by determining the strategic need and strategic Outcomes (stages 0.3 and 0.4).

Stage 0.2 consists of the following activities:

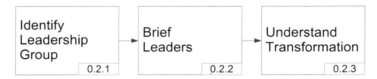

Figure II.0.3 – Activities in stage 0.2 – Engage leadership

0.2.1 Identify leadership group

Within this first activity, the Senior Responsible Owner, supported by the phase 0 team, needs to discuss the transformation potential within different areas of the business. These may be areas where leaders foresee opportunities in the future because of forthcoming changes, such as changes in technology, legislation or customer expectations. It may include areas for innovation which will drive the business forward or where there are difficulties that need to be resolved. Leaders may have seen change in other organisations and feel that there is scope for dramatic improvement within their own business.

These discussions need to happen at the highest level, for example, with an executive management team, strategic directors, stakeholders, trustees or elected members within a local authority. The representatives from these groups should form the leadership group for transformation initiation. In addition, there should be subject matter experts involved who help leaders to initiate transformational change and facilitate discussions.

0.2.2 Brief leaders

When leaders of the transformation initiation have been identified, preparation for the discussions can start. The first step is a series of briefings by the Senior Responsible Owner that outline the need for change within the organisation and areas of interest that could be explored further. The briefings may also cover the potential Outcomes within these areas.

0.2.3 Understand transformation

In addition to understanding the opportunities for change within their organisation, the leadership team should review the concept of transformational change and the magnitude of the change they might be embarking on.

Unlike process improvement, transformational change is not just about 'How can we do what we do better/cheaper/faster?' It is about asking a more fundamental question:

'Why do we do what we do at all?'

Transformational change information gathering could involve:

- Benchmarking visits to best practice examples in other organisations
- Visits to organisations that have undertaken transformational change
- Facilitated sessions with leading academics and subject matter experts.

At the end of this information gathering leaders should be able to answer questions such as:

- What is transformational change?
- What could be achieved?
- What is the likely impact?
- What is in it for me?

0.3 DETERMINE STRATEGIC NEED

Purpose

What is driving transformational change?

Before embarking on transformation, leaders should understand the need for change. Transformation can be viewed as a journey from strategic needs, to the strategic Outcomes.

Figure II.0.4 – Linking strategic need to strategic Outcome

There are many reasons for transformational change, from addressing issues in the business to exploring opportunities. These reasons should be formulated into a strategic need, so that it will be quite clear what the leaders are trying to address.

Stage 0.3 consists of the following activities:

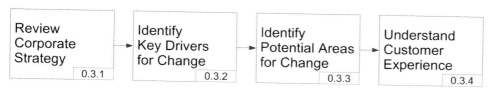

Figure II.0.5 – Activities in stage 0.3 – Determine strategic need

0.3.1 Review corporate strategy

The starting point for identifying the strategic need and assessing the organisation's transformation potential is a review of corporate strategy. There are a number of questions leaders might want to ask.

- Is there an up-to-date strategy?

■ Does the strategy still meet leaders' aspirations?
■ Does the strategy meet the external demands on the business?
■ To what extent is the current business aligned to this strategy?
■ Where are the greatest gaps between the current business and the strategy?
■ Are current change initiatives aligned to this strategy?

Once the alignment with corporate strategy has been assessed, the key business drivers for change should be explored.

0.3.2 Identify key drivers for change

There may be a number of business drivers for change within the business area. The purpose of this activity is to identify and understand the key internal and external change drivers.

The internal change drivers may include:
■ Improving customer satisfaction
■ Efficiency savings
■ An increase in demand for products or services
■ Opportunities and issues with the current business
■ Improving profit
■ Stakeholder preferences.

The external change drivers may include:
■ Legislation changes
■ Government initiatives
■ Economic conditions
■ Social changes/demographics – the way we live and work
■ Technology changes – for example, how we integrate with business and social networks
■ Local, national and global outlook – such as competition from other organisations or sectors.

0.3.3 Identify potential areas for change

Which business areas should be included within the transformational change?

To maximise the change potential, every effort should be made at this stage to keep the scope of transformation, as wide as possible and to break the boundaries between current services, functions or organisation units. It is worth thinking outside of the current organisation structure and to consider collaboration or joint working. Alternatively, it may be useful to think outside of the current customer base and current service or product offerings.
The business area(s) identified within this activity form a provisional scope for transformational change and will be explored further in the activities which follow.

Business area
A business area, in the context of transformational change, does not necessarily refer to a distinct section of the current organisation. It may cover a number of services, or an aspect of the organisation that cuts across many sections, such as information management.

0.3.4 Understand customer experience

In addition to identifying the key business drivers (stage 0.3), it is vital to look closely at the key customer groups and to identify what their expectations and their measures of success will be.

The questions to be answered at this stage are:
- What is the current customer experience?
- What are customers' expectations?
- What are they being offered by similar organisations?
- What is important to them?
- How will customers measure the success of transformational change?
- What will be their judgement criteria?
- What do they say they want?
- What do they need?

The team also needs to look into the future and understand the future trends, rising or different customer expectations, and changing needs.

Business drivers, along with these customer experience drivers, contribute to the development of the strategic needs which will go into the Strategic Business Case.

0.4 DETERMINE STRATEGIC OUTCOMES

Purpose

What will be the result of change?

Once the strategic need for transformational change has been established, the emphasis in thinking now shifts to the future and the desired Outcomes of transformational change. Strategic Outcomes express the leaders' ambition for change. They form the basis for defining more detailed Outcomes within phase 1 – Visioning. The key inputs into defining strategic Outcomes are the business drivers and customer experience drivers.

Stage 0.4 consists of the following activities:

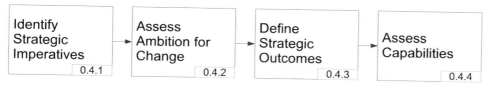

Figure II.0.6 – Activities for stage 0.4 – Determine strategic Outcomes

0.4.1 Identify strategic imperatives

Leaders need to determine and agree upon the priorities. In other words, what are the critical changes that need to happen? These contribute directly to the strategic Outcomes (stage 0.4.3) and should form the basis of the Future Operating Model (stage 1.5).
- The most important priority areas ('must haves') of the business should be identified and expressed as business area imperatives. These are the business areas that MUST be changed if the customer experience and business drivers, defined within stage 0.3, are to be met

■ The most important business processes ('must dos') that each business area must focus upon should be identified and expressed as process imperatives. These will be the business processes that MUST be changed and improved.

The appropriate number of transformational change imperatives will vary, but for most programmes between two and four will be sufficient.

0.4.2 Assess ambition for change
Leaders' ambition for change will, to a large extent, affect the strategic Outcomes. A business area with more limited aims will thus have a lower potential to generate transformation Benefits. Ambition for change will be shaped by:
■ Drivers for change (stage 0.3)
■ Customer experience (stage 0.3)
■ Business area and process imperatives (stage 0.4)
■ Other examples of what might be possible from transformation information gathering (stage 0.2).

Each business area needs to be assessed for the level of service or product it is aiming to provide and the magnitude of the remodelling required. Not all business areas will aim for, or need to be, 'world class' or strive for extensive change: some may need more basic improvement. The information is used to define the strategic Outcomes.

0.4.3 Define strategic Outcomes
The purpose of this activity is to define strategic Outcomes that express leaders' objectives for the business in a simple set of statements, matching the strategic need.

Strategic Outcomes
The high-level results of change that affect customers, employees, the organisation and stakeholders. For example, a revitalised economy, higher position in the market place.

The key inputs into developing strategic Outcomes are the change drivers identified in stage 0.3, the business imperatives from stage 0.4 and the ambition for change expressed in stage 0.4.

Strategic Outcomes, at a high level, define the effect of transformational change on:
■ Customers
■ Employees
■ Efficiency.

And, in turn, this rewards stakeholders, for example, by offering greater return on investment.

The aim may be to achieve:
■ **Perception of excellence by customers**
  This may mean changes within the organisation which enable a fast and accurate response to customers, a choice of channels of communication, and services that are tailored to customers' needs.

■ **Customer-facing culture**
This may mean making changes in the organisation which give employees greater levels of empowerment, more advanced tools to deal with customer queries and a better reward structure.

■ **Highly efficient operation**
This may mean removing duplication of effort, streamlining processes, cutting costs or ensuring accurate information is available.

Strategic Outcomes, together with the strategic need, form a key part of the Strategic Business Case. Strategic Outcomes also form the basis for defining detailed Outcomes within phase 1 – Visioning.

0.4.4 Assess capabilities

To achieve the strategic Outcomes (identified within stage 0.4), it is necessary to review the key capabilities that exist now and to consider what will need to be in place in the future in terms of business processes, organisation structure, people, facilities, properties, technology and so on. Leaders can then review the gap and identify any new capabilities. It is this gap that needs to be addressed by the transformational change programme.

The cost of moving from current to future capabilities forms the basis for arriving at an indicative cost in stage 0.5.3. It should also be possible at this stage to assess the impact on the business.

0.5 DEVELOP THE STRATEGIC BUSINESS CASE

Purpose

Is there a case for transformation?
Within this stage, the strategic need, the strategic Outcomes and the aspirations of leaders for the business area are documented in the Strategic Business Case.

Strategic Business Case
A high-level Business Case which articulates the strategic need and strategic Outcomes and determines the strategic Benefits versus indicative costs.

Stage 0.5 consists of the following activities:

Figure II.0.7 – Activities for stage 0.5 – Develop the Strategic Business Case

0.5.1 Outline transformation scope

The initial scope for transformation can be determined from the early exploration of potential areas for change in stages 0.2.2 and 0.3.3.

It is important to keep the scope as broad as possible at this stage to enable truly transformational thinking during visioning. This scope forms the basis for further exploration of transformation potential within phase 1– Visioning, and phase 2 – Shaping and Planning, and will be refined several times before the scope of the actual transformation programme is decided.

0.5.2 Define strategic Benefits

The success of transformational change is measured by the Benefits it delivers. It is the Benefits that drive the transformational change journey.

Strategic Benefit
The strategic Benefit is the ultimate difference the transformation will make to customers, the organisation, employees and stakeholders.

It will be translated into a series of measurable Benefits in phase 2, that will be used to prove that strategic Benefits have been achieved.

The justification for undertaking any transformational change programme is that there are Benefits to be won. If there aren't any Benefits, there's no point in embarking on the programme. At this stage the Benefits are defined only at strategic level. In other words, outline the types of Benefits to be delivered with indicative values and an indicative level of confidence in achieving them, rather than producing detailed definitions with accurate estimates.

Benefits should be sought in three areas:
- Benefits to customers, such as improvements in customer satisfaction, quality improvements to goods and reduction in transaction times
- Benefits to employees, such as better tools and equipment to do their job and improved working environment
- Efficiency savings, such as cost reduction.

Benefits to wider stakeholders should also emerge as a result, such as revenue generation, cost avoidance and the achievement of mandatory legislative or regulatory requirements.

There is a chapter about Benefits management in section III.

0.5.3 Determine indicative costs

The indicative costs of the proposed transformational change are based on the new capabilities that are required to deliver the strategic Outcomes. To identify what needs changing and where the investment is needed, it is important to start from Strategic Outcomes and work back to the Strategic Benefits.

It is common for organisations to start with the solution and then look for the Benefits that justify it, but this is a fundamental flaw and often a reason that change initiatives fail.

Once the required outputs have been identified, the indicative costs can be estimated from a number of sources, such as past experience, learning from other organisations, estimates from third-party suppliers, change impact and so on.

Apart from the total cost of transformation, there needs to be a focus on the most cost-effective areas. The perceived value of the strategic Outcomes should be aligned against the likely cost of delivering them.

0.5.4 Complete Strategic Business Case

The Strategic Business Case consolidates the information from the whole of phase 0. It is the first stage of the Business Case development process and will be followed by an Outline Business Case within phase 1 and Full Business Case in phase 2.

The purpose of the Strategic Business Case is to communicate leaders' aspirations for transformational change and define the strategic need and strategic Outcomes that will set the start and end points for the transformational change journey.

Transformational change typically requires a large investment, long time scales, as well as having a significant impact on the business and requiring approval at the highest level (stage 0.6).

Below, you will see an outline of what is covered in the Strategic Business Case and how it fits into the transformation journey.

Product title	Strategic Business Case (SBC)	Phase 0
Purpose	To identify the strategic need for change and set strategic Outcomes	
Description	The Strategic Business Case communicates leaders' aspirations for transformational change and defines the strategic need and strategic Outcomes that will set the start and end points for the transformation journey. It also provides an initial justification for transformational change based on strategic Benefits and indicative costs	
Composition	■ Scope/area of interest ■ Strategic need ■ Strategic Outcomes ■ Strategic Benefits ■ Indicative cost ■ Indicative timescales	
Input from	Corporate strategies	
Used as an input to	Vision, Future Operating Model, Outline Business Case	
Approved by	Executive gate	

Table II.0.1 – Strategic Business Case composition

0.5.5 Agree approach to change management

Once the Strategic Business Case has been written, leaders will have a clearer view of the magnitude of change. Right from the outset leaders need to start thinking about how to build support and overcome resistance within the organisation and agree some key principles that will drive future change management activities. The approach should suit the organisation in which they are to be used, but leaders may consider:

- Emphasising the inevitability of change
- Persuasion
- Rewards
- Compromises and bargaining
- Guarantees against personal loss, for example, offering job security or retraining
- Employee participation
- Building loyalty and a sense of ownership
- Gradual implementation of change.

Getting the widest possible participation is a particularly effective way of developing ownership, willingness to share information and co-operation through the whole change lifecycle.

The approach to change management starts here, at a high level. It is developed throughout CHAMPS2 to ensure that people understand what will happen to them, their customers and the business and, if possible, that they feel committed to change. The change management approach is supported by regular activities concerned with communication and consultation.

0.6 EXECUTIVE GATE

Purpose

During this stage, the Strategic Business Case is submitted for Executive approval. The Executive will assess the proposal and make a decision as to whether to take it further and develop an Outline Business Case.

Stage 0.6 consists of the following activities:

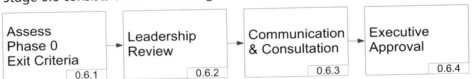

Figure II.0.8 – Activities in stage 0.6 – Executive gate

0.6.1 Assess Phase 0 Exit Criteria

At the end of the phase the Quality Assurance Function will perform an end-of-phase review, using the Phase Exit Criteria Checklist. The Checklist describes the outcomes that are expected from the particular phase – irrespective of the actual approach used. The criteria contained in all the Phase Exit Criteria Checklists are listed in appendix 2.

The Checklist asks for evidence of how the criteria have been met. Against each of the criteria, the Quality Assurance Function, having reviewed the evidence, will record an overall quality assessment using a red/amber/green (RAG) method.

Once the Phase Exit Criteria Checklist has been completed, the key learning points should be identified and made available to other programmes and projects in the form of lessons learnt.

0.6.2 Leadership review

The Strategic Business Case is likely to have been built over several meetings and workshops with the phase 0 team. Leaders now need to review the document to determine:

- Whether it presents a strong case
- The potential scope of transformation
- Strategic Outcomes versus strategic need
- Strategic Benefits versus indicative costs.

0.6.3 Communication and consultation

Communication to stakeholders is important in all phases of CHAMPS2. This activity should focus on the latest decisions and developments that affect them, as well as outlining the next steps to manage their expectations.

Communication will help people to understand what to expect and what is expected of them. Consider how change will affect employees, customers, suppliers and stakeholders. Effective communication is only really possible where there is an understanding of each group's perspective.

In phase 0, leaders need to communicate clearly their commitment to strategic change and the potential improvements for employees, customers and stakeholders. Messages should provide information on what has happened so far and what will be happening next.

A period of consultation may also be required. The Strategic Business Case should be submitted to stakeholders for consultation. This will vary from organisation to organisation and may include for example:

- **Consultation with customers and interested parties**
  This could include performance, efficiency and IT groups, a range of customers and employees, business functions, partner businesses and so on.

- **Consultation with stakeholders**
  Consultation with stakeholders such as suppliers, shareholders, customers, directors, elected members or trustees is important to ensure that the needs of those with a vested interest in the future are addressed.

- **Consultation with trade unions**
  Transformational change invariably affects people, both customers and employees. A meeting with trade unions may be needed to discuss potential implications for the organisation's structure and staffing levels, and changes to jobs or relocations.

- **Consultation with Quality Assurance**
  It is also useful to include consultation with the Quality Assurance Function, who will oversee the process and use of the CHAMPS2 method.

0.6.4 Executive approval

Once consultations are complete, the Strategic Business Case is submitted for Executive approval. Depending on the type of organisation this may mean approval by a Board of Directors or, for a Local Authority, this would be the Cabinet or one of its committees.

The objective of the approval is for Executives to assess the strategic Outcomes and strategic Benefits against the indicative cost, and to decide on funding options. The aim is to agree potential funding for the whole change initiative and approve the funding for phase 1. The Executives will also assess the effect of the proposed transformational change within the context of other transformational change programmes or other initiatives within the organisation.

Once the Strategic Business Case has been approved, the transformation can proceed to phase 1 – Visioning.

PHASE 0 SUMMARY

Phase 0 is used to make a 'space' for the new transformation initiative. In this phase, leaders of the organisation:

- Determine the strategic need for transformation
- Formulate the strategic Outcomes
- Determine the strategic Benefits.

Indicative costs of transformation are also determined and funding options considered. The information is documented within the Strategic Business Case.

Hints and tips

Transformational change

It may be helpful to note that unlike process improvement, transformational change is not just about 'How can we do what we do better/cheaper/faster?', but is about asking a more fundamental question:

'Why do we do what we do at all?'

It may involve remodelling processes, IT systems or the organisation itself, but fundamentally it is about responding effectively to opportunities to transform your business.

Reflective questions

Reflective questions require you to examine your existing knowledge or experience before giving a thoughtful response.

Phase 0 makes a 'space' for the new transformation initiative, and that means understanding the drivers for change, its scope, and the customer experience.

1. Consider and compare: (a) the main aspirations and drivers for change in your organisation, (b) the customer experience now, (c) what the customer experience could look like.

2. Take this opportunity to explore your own attitude to change. When faced with change do you, for example, feel positive about the opportunities or negative about the disruption? Can you think of any elements of your own job or work area that you would not like to change? What would your reaction be if you had to change to a new way of working?

3. Can you think of any examples of difficulties you have had in trying to implement change in the past? What are the key opportunities for change in your part of the business?

Phase 1 – Visioning

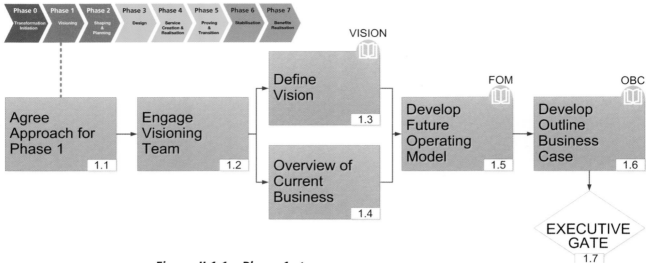

Figure II.1.1 – Phase 1 stages

Phase 1

Visioning sets the targets for transformational change and examines how the organisation could work in the future.

PURPOSE OF PHASE 1 – VISIONING

Visioning sets the targets for the transformation of a particular business area by:

- Formulating a Vision statement encompassing the ultimate targets for the business. For example, what the business could be like in the future, how it will feel, look or seem different to a customer
- Developing specific Outcomes that the business area wishes to achieve to move towards its Vision
- Developing a Future Operating Model that describes the high level composition and operation of the changed organisation that will deliver the desired Outcomes.

At the end of this phase the Outline Business Case is created, setting the direction for transformation. It also provides a justification for the development of a Full Business Case.

ROLES AND RESPONSIBILITIES

Executive – Approve the direction expressed in the Outline Business Case and decide whether to make the investment.

Visioning team – Agree the Vision, ensure the Outcomes are truly transformational and agree how the organisation will work in the future – the Future Operating Model.

Phase 1 team – Facilitate visioning, develop the Future Operating Model and produce the Outline Business Case.

Design Authorities – Review and have an input into process, organisation and technology aspects of the Future Operating Model.

Quality Assurance Function – This group continues to provide advice and to monitor quality and the use of CHAMPS2.

1.1 AGREE APPROACH FOR PHASE 1

Purpose

All transformational change is different and to cater for this it is possible to tailor CHAMPS2 to suit individual needs. Tailoring involves reviewing the path towards change through the various stages and agreeing the approach you want to take.

Stage 1.1 consists of the following activities:

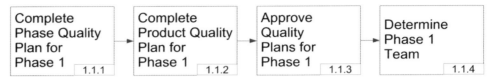

Figure II.1.2 – Activities in stage 1.1 – Agree approach for phase 1

1.1.1 – 1.1.3 Quality Plans

The approach for phase 1 is captured in two documents that are central to maintaining quality standards and managing client expectations:

- **Phase Quality Plan** – to tailor the stages and activities to the programme's needs
- **Product Quality Plan** – to ensure the quality of each product and how it is approved.

At the end of the phase the **Phase 1 Exit Criteria Checklist** should be used to assess whether the phase objectives have been met. This document, therefore, forms a vital input into the development of Quality Plans and should be considered when they are being created. Lessons learnt from phase 0 and from other change initiatives should be considered when choosing the most appropriate approach.

The Phase and Product Quality Plans and Exit Criteria Checklist are key products from the Quality Management Framework which is fully explained in section III.

1.1.4 Determine phase 1 team

Defining the future requires a phase 1 team to facilitate sessions and get to grips with the current customer experience and customer expectations, as well as the hopes and fears of people in all the business areas involved. The team should:

- Support managers to understand transformation and ensure the Outcomes are truly transformational
- Carry out interviews and workshops with managers to capture their hopes and fears
- Facilitate visioning workshops
- Collate information about customers' experiences and expectations
- Work with the visioning team and business managers to consolidate the information into the required documents.

The role of this team is to document the Vision and Future Operating Model, which are created by the visioning team. It is important that the team has a good understanding of what the business area does, as well as of the existing

- Describes a compelling future
- Avoids target dates, unless it is truly time dependant
- Is verifiable without too many targets.

The Vision statement expresses an ultimate, and not necessarily realistic, goal for transformational change. To counter-balance this it is also necessary to focus on specific Outcomes expected within different business areas.

1.3.6 Develop detailed Outcomes

Outcomes should be clear, specific and contain objectives and metrics where possible. Unlike the Vision statement, the Outcomes should be realistic and achievable. They will be used later to identify Benefits.

An **Outcome** is a result of change and its effect on customers, employees, efficiency or stakeholders.

Outcomes are typically linked to specific services and customer groups. Therefore, the development of Outcomes should be performed by individual business areas based on:
- The Vision statement
- Strategic Outcomes
- Customer experience drivers
- Business area imperatives
- Real world constraints.

Together the Outcomes and Vision statement are used to create the Vision.

Product title	Vision		Phase 1
Purpose	To set the target for transformational change		
Description	The Vision is an externally facing image of the future, describing what the change will achieve. It consists of an overarching Vision statement and a set of concrete Outcomes for different customer groups, employees or financial results		
Composition	■ Vision statement ■ Outcomes		
Input from	Strategic Business Case		
Used as an input to	Future Operating Model, Outline Business Case, Full Business Case		
Approved by	Executive (as part of the Outline Business Case)		

Table II.1.1 – Vision composition

1.4 OVERVIEW OF THE CURRENT BUSINESS

Purpose

What is the current state of the business?

Whilst the Vision and desired Outcomes outline where the business wants to be in the future, this stage explores where the business is now and what difference can be made. This will enable the business to identify the priority areas that need to be changed and make clearer judgements about how much it will cost.

Different aspects of the business are investigated, including the organisation structure, processes, technology, performance, and current projects and initiatives. It is important not to spend too much time on this activity. Detailed mapping is not only time consuming, but also potentially constrains creative thinking.

Stage 1.4 consists of the following activities:

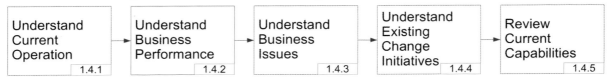

Figure II.1.5 – Activities in stage 1.4 – Overview of the current business

1.4.1 Understand current operation

The purpose of this series of activities is to understand how the current business operates and the strengths and weaknesses of current operations. Business issues, existing business initiatives and capabilities are also explored. They fall into three broad areas.

Processes

Create an overview of each process and its interfaces with other processes. This activity is NOT concerned with detailed process mapping. Explore, instead, process effectiveness and efficiency and how well processes align to organisational strategy.

Organisation

Capture the current infrastructure, locations and organisation charts to gain a high-level understanding of the functions performed by different organisation units. Explore the management of the business area, including decision-making processes, controls that are in place, key roles and responsibilities, lines of reporting, skills, capacity and the overall culture.

Technology

Review the technology, such as hardware and software platforms, networks or database platforms and list the key applications with basic details – for example: functionality, platform, performance, reliability, volume of usage or current support arrangements.

1.4.2 Understand business performance
Information on the business area's performance metrics and high-level costs should also be gathered. This will help to calculate and measure Benefits. Performance is measured by a set of indicators with pre-defined targets, such as customer satisfaction, meeting delivery targets, resource utilisation.

1.4.3 Understand business issues
It should be clear how the business area's performance metrics affect the main organisation's performance metrics and any issues that may prevent the business area meeting its targets. For example:
- Lack of funding
- Insufficient capacity to cope with customer demands
- Unreliable ICT infrastructure
- Skills shortages.

Even if the business area is meeting its targets, there may be other issues, such as:
- Communication problems
- Conflicts between departments
- Quality problems
- Inefficiencies
- Low employee morale
- Location problems.

1.4.4 Understand existing change initiatives
There could also be other transformation programmes, non-transformational projects, legal or regulatory changes or other initiatives in the business area which could overlap. The combined change impact needs to be taken into consideration when scoping the transformation or it may be necessary to stop some of the current initiatives. Therefore, these need to be identified, their objectives understood and their status documented.

1.4.5 Review current capabilities
A review of capabilities and performance will inform the development of the Outline Business Case (stage 1.6) and will help to prioritise the changes according to the greatest capability gap. When it is known what needs to be changed, then the cost of transformation can be more accurately judged.

The review could include:
- The organisation structure and accountabilities
- Skills, capacity and culture
- Process effectiveness and efficiency
- Organisation alignment to processes
- Technology
- Data accuracy, availability and ownership
- Infrastructure and property.

1.5 DEVELOP FUTURE OPERATING MODEL (FOM)

Purpose

How will the business work in the future to deliver the desired Outcomes and ultimately the Vision? How does that differ from current operations?

Future Operating Model

The Future Operating Model (FOM) is a high-level document that describes the key components of the future organisation, including the key processes, organisation structure and technology platforms. It demonstrates the way in which the organisation has to change in order to deliver the Outcomes.

Stage 1.5 consists of the following activities:

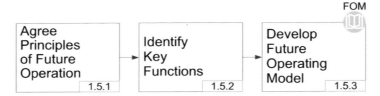

Figure II.1.6 – Activities in stage 1.5 – Develop Future Operating Model

1.5.1 Agree principles of future operation

The guiding principles for the Future Operating Model should reflect the leaders' philosophy about the business. They will typically cover customer service, performance management, leadership style, culture and behaviours, relationship with employees, ethics, social responsibilities and so on.

For example, the service may change from:
- Reactive to preventative, for example, planning building maintenance rather than reacting to problems
- Entitlement-based to needs based, for example, in providing social care
- Product-driven to customer-driven, for example, providing the services and products required by customers
- Opt-in principle to opt-out principle, for example, a service continues until cancelled.

The principles of future operation may include decisions on:
- The extent to which processes should be concentrated or fragmented
- Whether decision-making should be done centrally or delegated
- Whether multiskilled or specialist jobs are required and what levels of empowerment should be sought.

The principles agreed at this stage will not only guide the development of the Future Operating Model, but will also form the basis for design principles used during Logical Design (in phase 2 – Shaping and Planning) and detailed design (in phase 3 – Design).

1.5.2 Identify key functions

Once the guiding principles have been agreed, the development of the Future Operating Model can be started. This involves:
- Identifying key components of the future business, such as a customer contact centre, customer research, service delivery

■ Defining the relationship between these components, for example, how the way customers are contacted informs knowledge about the customer
■ Identifying the key differences against the current operation. These will need to be emphasised when communicating the Future Operating Model – for example, a shift in the ownership of customer requests from back office teams to frontline staff.

The high-level Future Operating Model should be documented in a simple diagram showing the key components and relationships. This forms the basis for defining the capabilities in more detail.

1.5.3 Develop Future Operating Model (FOM)

Once key functions have been agreed, the Future Operating Model can be developed further to define the changes that need to be made to different aspects of the business:

Processes	Identify the key processes within the future operation. These will form the basis for process decomposition within phase 2 – Shaping and Planning.
Organisation	Define a conceptual organisational design which outlines the top levels of the organisation and describe how the principles such as centralisation versus delegation and multiskilled versus specialist jobs have been applied.
Technology	Outline the key technologies that will be needed to support the future operation.

The Future Operating Model may also describe other aspects of the business, for example, performance management, culture, or property.

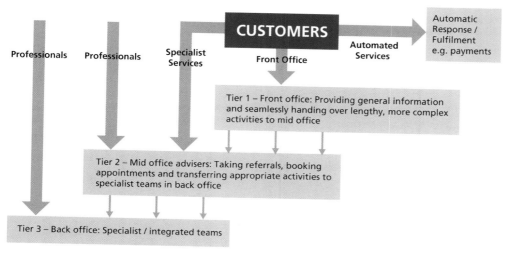

Figure II.1.7 – Example Future Operating Model

The aim, in this example, is to use specialist staff in the most appropriate way, with a few generalist staff in the front office. This is achieved with a three-tier model.

Different organisations will, of course, approach the change in different ways. For example, the organisation could aim to respond to the bulk of queries with generalist front office staff and only a few specialists in support.

So, what is covered in the Future Operating Model document?

Product title	Future Operating Model (FOM)	Phase 1
Purpose	To set the principles of the future operation	
Description	An internally facing image of the future, describing what the organisation will look like and how it will operate in order to achieve the Vision and desired Outcomes. This is the highest level of solution design, identifying key functions and key flows	

Composition	■ Principles of future operation
	■ A diagram showing key capabilities and relationships
	■ Aspects of future operation:
	  □ Processes
	  □ Organisation
	  □ Technology
	  □ Performance management
	■ How the Future Operating Model supports the Vision and Outcomes
	■ Requirements arising from the Future Operating Model	

Input from	Strategic Benefits	
Used as an input to	Logical Design	
Approved by	Process Design Authority, Organisation Design Authority, Technology Architecture Authority, Programme Board	

Table II.1.2 – Future Operating Model composition

The Future Operating Model is a key document that drives the Logical Design and solution selection within phase 2 – Shaping and Planning, and detailed design within phase 3 – Design.

1.6 DEVELOP OUTLINE BUSINESS CASE (OBC)

Purpose

Where does the business want to go in the future?

The focus of the Outline Business Case is on what transformation is going to achieve. At this stage costs and timescales are only indicative. It presents an initial perspective on the scope of transformation, together with the high-level Benefits.

Stage 1.6 consists of the following activities:

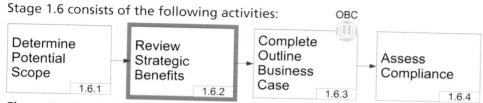

Figure II.1.8 – Activities in stage 1.6 – Develop Outline Business Case

1.6.1 Determine potential scope

A number of activities and products within phase 1 so far have concentrated on describing the future:

- Vision statement
- Detailed Outcomes
- Future Operating Model.

All this information is now consolidated, the areas of focus identified and the next step is to determine the potential scope for transformation.

Scoping should focus on the elements of the Future Operating Model that deliver the vital Outcomes and achieve the highest Benefits. It may be that only 20% of activities will deliver 80% of the overall result. Concentrating on specific areas of the Future Operating Model may also make the transformation more feasible.

1.6.2 Review strategic Benefits and indicative costs

The strategic Benefits and indicative costs from phase 0 can also be reviewed. These Benefits and costs can now be estimated more accurately. They are, however, still only indicative figures, since no Benefits calculations, nor programme planning, have taken place at this stage.

The high-level Benefits form part of the justification for transformational change within the Outline Business Case. They also form the basis for identifying the more detailed SMART Benefits during phase 2 – Shaping and Planning.

1.6.3 Complete Outline Business Case

The phase 1 team consolidates the information into the Outline Business Case.

Outline Business Case

The Outline Business Case communicates clearly the direction for transformational change before any detailed design and planning take place. It also outlines the Benefits and indicative costs of transformation.

What is covered in the Outline Business Case?

Product title	Outline Business Case (OBC)	Phase 1
Purpose	To get approval for the direction of change, before the Full Business Case is developed	
Description	The Outline Business Case communicates the Vision and detailed Outcomes for the business area. It outlines the changes required and potential Benefits, and justifies the development of the Full Business Case	

Composition	■ Scope
	■ Need for change
	■ Strategic direction
	  □ Vision statement
	  □ Detailed Outcomes
	  □ Future Operating Model
	■ Change impact
	■ Indicative cost
	■ Indicative timescales
	■ High-level Benefits
	■ High-level risks
	■ Links with other change initiatives	

Input from	Strategic Business Case, Vision, Future Operating Model	
Used as an input to	Logical Design, Full Business Case	
Approved by	Executive gate	

Table II.1.3 – Outline Business Case composition

1.6.4 Assess compliance
The information contained within the Outline Business Case should be assessed to check whether it complies with legislation or any external or internal policies.

■ **Corporate strategies**
Alignment with corporate strategy should be examined, as well as compliance with any other internal strategies or policies. This would, for example, include strategies related to sustainability, carbon emissions management or ecological footprint.

■ **External policies**
This includes compliance with legislation, such as the Data Protection Act and any relevant external policies.

Benefits Realisation Board – Reviews the newly identified Benefits and judges whether they are realistic and challenging.

Programme Manager – Appointed in phase 2. Will structure and manage the programme, monitor its progress and manage risks, issues and interdependencies between projects.

Programme Team – Facilitates Logical Design, supplier selection, identification of Benefits and develops the Full Business Case.

Programme Board – Approves Logical Design and Product and Supplier Recommendation and reviews the Full Business Case.

Process Design Authority, Organisation Design Authority and Technology Architecture Authority – Review relevant aspects of Logical Design.

Executive – Approves the Full Business Case and releases funding for programme delivery.

Business Change Manager – Identifies Benefits alongside the Programme Team.

Quality Assurance Function – Provides advice and monitors both quality and the use of CHAMPS2.

2.1 AGREE APPROACH FOR PHASE 2

Purpose

It is possible to tailor the CHAMPS2 method to suit the needs of individual programmes. Tailoring involves reviewing the path through each of the relevant stages and agreeing the approach you want to take.

Stage 2.1 consists of the following activities:

Figure II.2.2 – Activities in stage 2.1 – Agree approach for phase 2

2.1.1 – 2.1.3 Quality Plans

The approach to phase 2 includes identifying aspects of CHAMPS2 to be included and those that will not be included. The approach will be captured in two documents that are central to maintaining quality standards and managing client expectations:

- **Phase Quality Plan** – to tailor the stages and activities to the programme's needs
- **Product Quality Plan** – to ensure the quality of each product and how it is signed off.

At the end of the phase, the Phase 2 Exit Criteria Checklist should be used to assess whether the phase objectives have been met. This document, therefore, forms a vital input into the development of Quality Plans and should be considered when they are being created. Lessons learnt from other change initiatives should be considered when choosing the most appropriate approach. These are key products from the Quality Management Framework, which is fully explained in section III.

2.1.4 Determine phase 2 team

A core phase 2 Programme Team needs to be set up to facilitate delivery of the Full Business Case. In addition, specialist teams and individuals need to be identified to get involved as and when required. The phase 2 team requires a number of key skills, including:

- Process designers for Logical Design
- Technology architects
- Organisation design specialists
- Procurement specialists to select suppliers for products
- Finance specialists to build viable cost Benefit cases
- Planners to develop project and programme plans.

This is often an appropriate point at which to begin considering what type of communications and consultation will be helpful during this phase, in preparation for the activity in stage 2.6.

2.2 DEFINE PROGRAMME SCOPE
Purpose
How big is the programme and what does it cover?
Whether the programme is large or small the boundaries need to be established for the transformational change programme before any planning can start.

- The programme scope should be agreed – what's in and what's out
- The objectives of the transformational change programme need to be defined
- High-level requirements for future service delivery need to be identified
- Measures of success for the transformational change programme are defined.

To ensure stakeholder buy-in throughout all activities, a stakeholder engagement plan is produced at this initial stage.

Stage 2.2 consists of the following activities:

Figure II.2.3 – Activities in stage 2.2 – Define programme scope

2.2.1 Define programme scope
The programme scope sets the boundaries for what is included in the programme and what is excluded, in terms of business areas, processes and deliverables. The scope is derived from the Future Operating Model, but the programme may choose not to attempt to deliver the full transformation and may focus on one particular aspect.

Without a clearly defined scope there is a risk of 'scope creep'. In other words, without a firm foundation for controlling changes to the programme it is likely to gradually drift away from its original objectives, timescales and budget.

The scope is based on the areas identified within the Future Operating Model and agreed in the Outline Business Case. The Future Operating Model sets the direction, but now attention needs to be focused on the areas where the highest Benefits can be realised. This should take into account the risks and costs.

There are a number of scope options, including to:
- Do the minimum to meet immediate business need
- Achieve some of the desired Outcomes
- Achieve/exceed the desired Outcomes.

The scope will be refined when the Full Business Case is developed and a careful balance is needed between costs and Benefits.

2.2.2 Define programme objectives

The programme objectives will be to deliver the Vision and desired Outcomes and realise Benefits at the end of the transformational journey. This will require the delivery of key capabilities which can be outlined at this stage. Additional objectives may be identified – for example, establishing partnerships, cultivating relationships, sharing knowledge, enabling other programmes or raising standards.

2.2.3 Develop stakeholder engagement plan

It is important to involve the stakeholders identified in phase 1 – Visioning, and others as required, to gain their buy-in and commitment to the programme. Stakeholders should feel that they are driving the change and that it is not 'being done to them'. Stakeholders may also provide help to design the most appropriate service delivery and programme delivery.

Engagement may range from giving stakeholders control, through working in partnership with stakeholders, to keeping stakeholders informed.

Activities could include:
- Agree high-level approach to stakeholder management
- Identify stakeholders
- Prioritise stakeholders
- Identify programme/project team 'owners' for each stakeholder
- Understand the key stakeholders
- Determine support required from each stakeholder, plus actions required
- Identify messages and actions required to win the support of stakeholders
- Regularly review status of key stakeholders and respond as necessary.

2.3 ANALYSIS OF CURRENT BUSINESS

Purpose

What does the business do?

Analysis of current business performance and capabilities builds on the information gathered in stage 1.4. It is important to focus on elements of the business that are targeted for transformation and only to the level of detail that will allow gaps to be assessed.

Where there are gaps in performance, Benefits could be delivered. Where there are gaps in capabilities, costs are likely to be incurred. Three aspects are explored: processes, organisation structure and technology.

The information gathered enables the Programme Team to identify Benefits and produce a programme plan with costings

Stage 2.3 consists of the following activities:

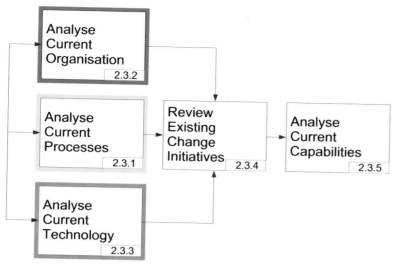

Figure II.2.4 – Activities in stage 2.3 – Analysis of current business

2.3.1 Analyse current processes

A basic understanding of current processes was documented in stage 1.4 – Overview of current business. Now the processes that are likely to be changed are analysed, detailing who does them and what technologies are used. Alongside process mapping, it is necessary to map the information flow and management information required.

- How much time is spent on each activity?
- How many people do it?
- How often do they do it?
- How many transactions are processed by each activity?

The result is the ability to calculate the cost of each activity within the process. These costs may provide a baseline for Benefits' definition.

2.3.2 Analyse current organisation

From the basic understanding of the organisation structure and functions gleaned in phase 1, further targeted analysis is required down to the job level, identifying the job titles, grades, roles and responsibilities and skills, including:

- Volumes (headcount and number of full-time equivalents (FTE))
- Cost analysis, either from budgetary perspective or salaries
- Overall strengths and weaknesses of the current organisation.

2.3.3 Analyse current technology

Technologies and application systems that need to change should be recorded with any technical specifications, version numbers and licence agreements. Any interfaces with systems outside the business area or external to the organisation need to be identified.

The reliability, performance, capacity, disaster recovery, business continuity arrangements, and current support arrangements are documented for any systems involved. The data held on systems also needs to be assessed, including:

■ Data models
■ Data storage and underlying technologies
■ Data volumes
■ Retention periods and archiving arrangements
■ Data quality: completeness, cleanliness, data integrity

The information gathered will help to assess the level of technological change required.

2.3.4 Review existing change initiatives

Some key initiatives have already been identified within stage 1.4 – Overview of current business. Mapping other initiatives will help us to avoid overlaps, incorporate or stop projects and programmes where necessary, and to understand the impact of change across the business. Within this activity a comprehensive list of initiatives is compiled, including:

■ Other transformation programmes affecting the business area
■ Continuous improvement projects
■ Campaigns
■ Organisation changes
■ Legislation changes affecting business area
■ Government initiatives.

2.3.5 Analyse current capabilities

This activity builds on the high-level capability assessment performed within stage 1.4 – Overview of current business. Capabilities need to be reviewed to assess how effective they are in the current business and then how suitable they would be within the future business.

A capability matrix is developed to align existing capabilities, such as processes, culture, staffing levels, infrastructure, technology and so on with the Future Operating Model. For example, the assessment may identify a strong sales function and skills base, but a weak technology infrastructure that does not match the Future Operating Model.

2.4 PREPARATION FOR LOGICAL DESIGN
Purpose
How do we get from the Future Operating Model to the design of the solution?

The design of the business solution evolves from the Future Operating Model in phase 1, through Logical Design in phase 2 to detailed design in phase 3. Preparation for Logical Design includes:

- Gathering the documents which define the principles to be used within, and the boundaries for, the Logical Design work
- Establishing a design environment, (both physical and technical)
- Ensuring that managers and design teams are fully trained.

Stage 2.4 consists of the following activities:

Figure II.2.5 – Activities in stage 2.4 – Preparation for Logical Design

2.4.1 Agree design principles
Design principles are required to make sure the design matches the culture, values, leadership style and policies of the organisation. There may already be a set of general design principles adopted by the organisation with which all programmes and projects have to comply.

In addition, specific design principles for the programme need to be agreed, for example, easy customer access to services, shortest service delivery time, minimum business impact. For each principle a measure of success should be defined that states 'what good looks like', such as customer access 24/7, service delivery within five days, a maximum of six layers of hierarchy in the organisation. These principles need to be balanced with constraints (such as time and cost) and will not necessarily seek a perfect solution but, rather, one that is acceptable.

2.4.2 Develop design framework
The design framework for Logical Design should ensure that the design teams and any subject matter experts brought in to assist with the design have the basic information to carry out Logical Design. It should document:

- Any requirements for the design identified in the Future Operating Model
- The high-level processes, organisation functions and technologies identified from the Future Operating Model
- The design principles
- The approach to be taken to the design, including the tools and techniques
- The products to be produced (also documented in Product Quality Plan).

The design framework also explains the roles and responsibilities during Logical Design and the design governance comprising three bodies: Process Design Authority, Organisation Design Authority and Technology Architecture Authority. There is more information about these roles in the governance chapter in section III.

2.4.3 Set up design environment

The physical environment used for design potentially needs to accommodate large numbers of people in design workshops. In the main, these workshops are used for process design. Workshops, break-out rooms and 'control rooms' that can be used throughout Logical Design may be required to maintain design wall charts, plans and so on.

A standard process design tool is advised for documenting processes and enabling their integration across work streams and other programmes.

2.4.4 Establish design teams

Separate process, organisation and technology design teams may need to be established. The process design team may be structured further into a number of work streams, which include the following roles:

- Process owners: client responsible for a particular process
- Subject matter experts: ensuring the quality of design
- Integration manager: ensuring that individual process designs integrate within and across programmes.

The process design team may also include change team members and technical consultants.

Finally, the design team should be trained to carryout Logical Design and document the results using the process design tool. The training needs to focus on a good understanding of the process and results of Logical Design including:

- The difference between Logical and detailed Design
- Process modelling method, for example, IDEF0
- Process decomposition
- Identifying inputs, outputs and controls
- Creation of process maps
- Using templates
- Integration of process maps.

2.5 LOGICAL DESIGN

Purpose

What processes, organisation structure and technology do we need?

Logical Design defines what processes and sub-processes will make up the service, their inputs and outputs, and the controls or policies that govern them. Alongside processes, a high-level organisation structure is defined and supporting technology identified. This is where the 'building blocks' of the new business solution are defined and set down.

■ **External policies**

This will include compliance with legislation, such as the Data Protection Act and any relevant external policies.

■ **Equality**

Equality assessment is one crucial part of compliance assessment that helps to determine whether the new service meets the standard equality criteria in relation to race, disability, gender, faith, age and sexual orientation.

A formal equality impact/needs assessment (EINA) should be carried out at this point to ensure that the newly designed solution, including process, organisation and technology, meets the needs of different groups within the community and will not have any discriminatory outcomes. For example, it is important to ensure that new technologies are actually useable by customers or employees with a disability.

2.5.10 Review strategic Benefits

Does the Logical Design support the strategic Benefits in the Outline Business Case? The review of Benefits involves comparing the newly designed processes with existing processes to see what differences in performance can be made. For example, there may be changes to Benefits arising from introducing a particular process into the design, or removing a process that hindered the current operation.

Benefits will be fully defined after product and supplier selection (stage 2.7).

2.6 PROGRAMME BOARD GATE

Purpose

Does the design match our needs?

Logical Design shows at high level what the solution will look like. At this point the Programme Board has to assess whether the programme is going in the right direction.

Stage 2.6 consists of the following activities:

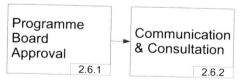

Figure II.2.7 – Activities in stage 2.6 – Programme Board gate

2.6.1 Programme Board approval

The Programme Board will review whether the design is likely to:

■ Deliver the desired Outcomes
■ Maximise the potential Benefits
■ Comply with the design principles and other requirements, such as equalities.

The change impact on the organisation should also be reviewed.

When, and if, the Programme Board approve the Logical Design, the programme can move on to select products and suppliers.

2.6.2 Communication and consultation

Communication to stakeholders is important in all phases of CHAMPS2. This activity should focus on the latest decisions and developments that affect them, as well as outlining the next steps to manage their expectations.

Communication and the impact of the Logical Design should be considered carefully. Any implications for staff and customers should be communicated, as appropriate.

A period of consultation may also be required. The Logical Design document should be submitted for consultation by stakeholders.

2.7 PRODUCT AND SUPPLIER SELECTION

Purpose

What technology and services do we need to buy in?

The purpose of this stage is to select the technology or external services that will support the processes identified during Logical Design. Outlined below is a typical procurement process. However, individual organisations may have standard or established processes that may be used.

Stage 2.7 consists of the following activities:

Figure II.2.8 – Activities in stage 2.7 – Product and supplier selection

2.7.1 Formulate business requirements

To select a suitable product or supplier, business requirements need to be defined first. Requirements are derived from the Future Operating Model and the Logical Design.

They should be formulated in terms of outcomes or outputs wherever possible, concentrating on what the business needs to deliver, rather than how it is to be delivered. This challenges suppliers and gives them the scope to develop innovative solutions.

2.7.2 Define selection criteria

The priorities need to be set for selecting the right supplier and the right solution/service. Depending on what the business wishes to achieve (defined within the design principles and the Logical Design), the emphasis for the solution/service selection may be on price, quality, experience, reliability, capacity, financial security and so on. The qualitative and financial element of the proposals should be evaluated separately, and then the two strands of the evaluation should be looked at together.

2.7.3 Identify products and suppliers

Suppliers should be checked to see whether they are on approved supplier lists where applicable. Their track record, financial stability and past experience with the supplier or recommendations can also be taken into account.

Potential suppliers should be sent business requirements and asked to complete a request for information or a pre-qualification questionnaire to provide further details about the company and the products or services.

2.7.4 Select product and supplier

Suppliers may be shortlisted first or an invitation to tender (ITT) document (or where an existing service provider is in place: a request for service) can be produced and sent out to the identified suppliers outlining the:
- Instructions, deadline, format and conditions for submitting responses
- Selection criteria.

With all of the supplier and/or service providers responses analysed, a recommendation for selection should be produced. This recommendation is then presented to the Programme Board for approval.

Product title	Product and Supplier Recommendation		Phase 2
Purpose	To select external products or service providers		
Description	The document presents the findings of the product and supplier evaluation and makes recommendations based on predefined selection criteria		
Composition	■ Business requirements ■ Shortlisted products and suppliers ■ Evaluation criteria ■ Evaluation results ■ Financial assessment ■ Recommendation		
Input from	Future Operating Model, Logical Design		
Used as an input to	Detailed design, Full Business Case		
Approved by	Programme Board		

Table II.2.2 – Product and Supplier Recommendation composition

2.8 PROGRAMME BOARD GATE

Purpose

Have we selected the right products and services?

Selection of technology and its supplier, or selection of a service provider will add another layer of understanding to what the solution looks like. At this point it is useful for the Programme Board to assess whether the programme is going in the right direction.

Stage 2.8 consists of the following activities:

```
Programme
Board
Approval
              2.8.1
```

Figure II.2.9 – Activities in stage 2.8 – Programme Board gate

2.8.1 Programme Board approval
The Programme Board needs to decide whether the solution:
- Is likely to deliver the desired Outcomes
- Maximises the potential Benefits
- Complies with the design principles and other requirements, such as equalities
- Is likely to have an impact on costs, timescales or risks.

2.9 IDENTIFY BENEFITS
Purpose
What difference will we make?
A transformational change programme should aim to deliver Outcomes that make a significant difference to the business and its customers. This difference must be measurable and is referred to as a Benefit.

The purpose of this stage is to identify the Benefits, produce a Benefits inventory and define each Benefit on a Benefit Card.

Stage 2.9 consists of the following activities:

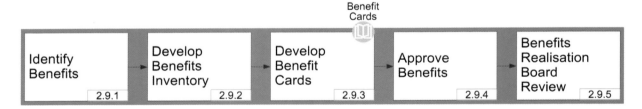

Figure II.2.10 – Activities in stage 2.9 – Identify Benefits

2.9.1 Identify Benefits

A Benefit is a measurable improvement resulting from an Outcome.

Benefits are identified by the Programme Team, together with Business Change Managers. They should be derived from specific Outcomes defined as part of the Vision in phase 1.

They should be measurable and contribute to the strategic Benefits documented in the Strategic Business Case.

Benefits are categorised as:
- Non-financial – for example, customer satisfaction, reputation
- Financial – such as an efficiency saving.

Financial Benefits can be further categorised as:
- Cashable – delivering the same for less money
- Non-cashable – delivering more for the same money

Apart from tangible Benefits, for example, financial savings or increased customer satisfaction, intangible Benefits should be considered. These are Benefits which cannot be measured, but will still contribute to the success of transformational change. These could be, for example, increased awareness or building relationships between different organisations.

2.9.2 Develop Benefits inventory

The Benefits inventory is used to list key Benefits. From a list of all of the Benefits, the less important ones should be weeded out and those priority ones that remain should be quantified. This is a vital stage – a value must be assigned to each Benefit. For example, 'the Benefit is a 10% saving which equates to a saving of £2 million per annum', or 'the Benefit is a 20% increase in customer satisfaction'. A way of measuring the Benefit should be suggested. This can be based on the organisation's own baseline data or on results from other organisations.

The objective is to concentrate measurement effort on the key Benefits. In other words, those which deliver the greatest share of financial savings or those which contribute most directly to the programme's objectives.

2.9.3 Develop Benefit Cards

Once listed and quantified, each Benefit is detailed on its own Benefit Card, which acts as a tracking vehicle and records Benefit status as Identified, Validated, Enabled and Realised. Each Benefit Card remains in existence until the Benefit is fully achieved (see section III chapter 3).

The main piece of information on the Benefit Card will be the value of the Benefit. This can be expressed, for example, as 'x% increase in customer satisfaction' or 'x amount of financial savings'.

Calculating financial Benefits involves:
- Establishing a measure base (for example, transaction cost, time spent on an activity)
- Calculating the Benefit for the base unit
- Calculating the annual value.

A level of confidence should be indicated against each Benefit – for example, 70%. This should increase as the level of understanding increases and the solution is developed.

The difference it will make if the estimates are incorrect, and how vulnerable the results are to a change in assumptions, should be estimated.

In addition, the Benefit Card contains the timescales for Benefits realisation and any dependencies or barriers that may potentially affect Benefits realisation. The status of the Benefits is set to Identified.

Product title	Benefit Card	Phase 2
Purpose	To define an individual Benefit and track its status	
Description	A separate Benefit Card is created for each Benefit and a Benefit Owner, who is responsible for realising the Benefit, is assigned,. The Benefit lifecycle is tracked on the Card, consisting of four states: ■ Identified ■ Validated ■ Enabled ■ Realised	

Composition	■ Benefit description
	■ Benefit type
	■ Value
	■ Benefit measures
	■ Baseline source
	■ Assumptions
	■ Dependencies
	■ Barriers to Benefits delivery
	■ Timings for Benefit realisation
	■ Benefit status: Identified, Validated, Enabled, Realised
	■ For each Benefit status:
	  ☐ Confidence in achieving the Benefit expressed as percentage
	  ☐ Date
	  ☐ Benefit Owner and signature	

Input from	Strategic Business Case, Outline Business Case	
Used as an input to	Full Business Case, Benefits Realisation Plan	
Approved by	Benefits Realisation Board, Benefit Owners	

Table II.2.3 – Benefit Card composition

2.9.4 Approve Benefits

Each Benefit Card needs to be assigned an owner. The Benefit Owner is typically a budget holder in the relevant business area. Whilst the Programme Team is responsible for enabling Benefits, the Benefit Owner will be accountable for realising the Benefit and will need to sign the Benefit Card through the Benefit lifecycle.

Benefit Owners need to fully understand the Benefit in terms of how it was calculated, where the savings/improvements will come from and how it can be achieved.

2.9.5 Benefits Realisation Board review

The Benefits Realisation Board needs to be aware of any newly identified Benefits, which areas they will be coming from, and their potential contribution towards total Benefits Realised within the organisation. At this stage they will be particularly looking to ensure that:

- The Identified Benefits are realistic
- There is no double counting of Benefits across different programmes or projects
- There is commitment to these Benefits within the business and each Benefit has a Benefit Owner.

The Benefits Realisation Board also needs to see the Benefits Realisation Plan once the programme planning has been completed.

2.10 DEVELOP THE PROGRAMME STRUCTURE

Purpose

How shall we structure the programme?

To make large programmes more manageable a structure of work streams and projects should be defined. The programme structure forms the basis for project and programme planning (stage 2.10) and the creation of appropriate programme governance (stage 2.11).

Stage 2.10 consists of the following activities:

Figure II.2.11 – Activities in stage 2.10 – Develop the programme structure

2.10.1 Identify programme overlaps

Links with other programmes, overlaps or dependencies should be identified before the programme is planned. The overlaps could be in a number of areas, for example, scope, stakeholders, resource, Benefits, technology or organisation. Ideally, they are resolved by dividing the responsibilities between the programmes and adjusting the scope of each programme.

To prevent double counting of Benefits, the ownership of Benefits has to be agreed and where necessary the value of the Benefit apportioned between programmes or projects.

2.10.2 Define programme delivery options

There are different approaches to structuring the programme and selecting the most suitable option. The programme structure can be driven, for example, by:

- Benefit groupings – all the capabilities required for a particular Benefit would be delivered together

- Capabilities – a particular capability delivered across different business areas
- Services – a group of related services are transformed together
- Geographical locations – transforming the business by geographical area.

Options should be evaluated based on Benefits, cost, timings and risks. In addition, there may be other criteria, such as resource implications or the impact of change.

Benefits driven programme structures are typically prioritised to deliver:
- Quick wins – to maintain stakeholder buy-in
- Financial Benefits – to fund the rest of transformation.

A phased approach could also be considered, or some of the programme delivery could be outsourced.

2.10.3 Develop programme structure

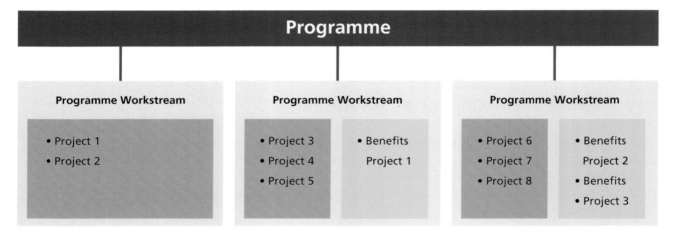

Figure II.2.12 – Structuring a programme into work streams and projects

Programmes can be structured into sub-programmes, work streams or projects. The scope and activities within the programme are assessed to see if they would be manageable as one piece of work or if it would be better to split them into more manageable chunks. Splitting a programme into work streams or projects means greater control over delivery, better management of risk, greater flexibility in reacting to change and greater visibility of real progress.

In addition to work streams and projects, the programme structure also needs to consider any cross-work stream activities that underpin programme delivery, for example, change management.

The projects identified within the programme structure may form a project portfolio. The projects can be further grouped into tranches according to the Benefits to which they contribute. At the end of each tranche a Benefits realisation project may need to be scheduled and added to the project portfolio. Different projects and tranches may be delivered at different times and so may be at different phases and stages in the CHAMPS2 lifecycle at the same time.

2.11.12 Develop Benefits management strategy

The Benefits management strategy describes how the programme is going to track Benefits and manage their delivery. It is needed to:

- Track Benefits: a mechanism to review which Benefit is in which status, the actual and anticipated value, and the achievement against target
- Provide a common approach to managing Benefits during development of the solution: how to ensure that the design aligns to Benefits; how to validate Benefits
- Provide a common approach to Benefits realisation: measuring; reporting
- Define roles and responsibilities in Benefits management and escalation process.

2.12 PROGRAMME PLANNING AND COSTING

Purpose

How long will it take and how much will it cost?

An overall programme plan should be produced, along with an estimate of the cost of the programme. The programme plan is based on high-level project plans for all projects within the project portfolio.

Breaking down the programme into a project portfolio means that each project can be planned independently. The projects are then integrated into an overall programme plan and the dependencies resolved.

Stage 2.12 consists of the following activities:

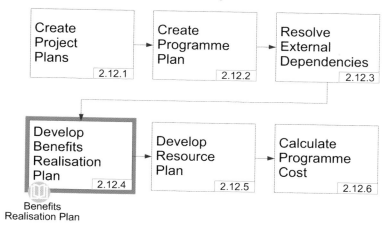

Figure II.2.14 – Activities in stage 2.12 – Programme planning and costing

2.12.1 Create project plans

In order to plan and cost the programme, the key products need to be identified for each project within the project portfolio. The list of products covers the whole programme lifecycle, from design to stabilisation, and is based on the standard products for phases 3 to 6.

The identified products are placed into a hierarchy to show which products are needed to build the final products. Then the sequence for the creation of all products needs to be determined and the dependencies between the products identified.

More detail should be added to create a critical path and milestones, and to estimate the duration of activities and resource requirements.

2.12.2 Create programme plan

The programme plan contains a high-level view of all the plans for the projects within the project portfolio and their key milestones and critical paths. Projects are grouped into tranches according to which Benefits they contribute. When a tranche is completed, the Outcomes should be reviewed and a Benefits project started.

Dependencies between projects within a programme should be established as well as critical paths and key milestones.

2.12.3 Resolve external dependencies

The integrated programme plan is further refined by adding the external dependencies such as third-party suppliers or other programmes.

It is vital that external dependencies are reduced where possible and the options for delivering them within the programme explored. This could involve reshaping the portfolio to limit the impact if the dependency is not delivered. External dependencies should be clearly highlighted in the plan and be included in the programme risk log with mitigating activities.

2.12.4 Develop Benefits Realisation Plan

In order to prove achievement of Benefits, they will need to be measured. This logically requires that baseline data is collected before implementation and then further data is collected during Benefits realisation. The Benefits Realisation Plan contains the milestones necessary to realise each Benefit and the details of events which prove that Benefits have been realised. This will include:

■ Collecting baseline data
■ Collecting new data
■ Evaluation
■ Delivery of the Benefits Realisation Report.

Any points where one programme intersects with other work streams or programmes should be identified and dependencies incorporated into the plan.

Product title	Benefits Realisation Plan		Phase 2
Purpose	To provide a timeline for Benefits realisation		
Description	A document showing timescales for different groups of Benefits and outlining the activities required to measure them		
Composition	■ Benefits list and expected values ■ Benefits realisation milestones ■ Activities required to measure Benefits		
Input from	Benefit Cards, programme plan		
Used as an input to	Full Business Case, Benefits Realisation Report		
Approved by	Benefits Realisation Board, Executive gate		

Table II.2.4 – Benefits Realisation Plan composition

2.12.5 Develop resource plan

The resource plan needs to be updated to include staff, assets and technology and service resources. Any resources required to control, track and govern the programme should be included.

Together with project resources, the programme resources need to be profiled over the duration of the programme to support the calculation of programme costings.

2.12.6 Calculate programme cost

Once there is clear understanding of resources required, the programme can be costed. For each member of staff or material resource profiled in the resource plan, a resource cost should be assigned.

When reviewing the programme scope, risks and issues, an appropriate contingency should be applied. Contingency can be calculated for risks and issues by multiplying the severity by a percentage of the total resource cost.

A change budget should also be identified, based on the confidence in the overall programme scope and anticipated change. This information should also be contained within the risk log.

2.13 DEVELOP THE FULL BUSINESS CASE (FBC)

Purpose

Is it worth it?

The purpose of this stage is to consolidate the information from the whole phase and develop a Full Business Case. This is the final stage of Business Case development that consists of:

■ Strategic Business Case, produced in phase 0

- Outline Business Case, produced in phase 1
- Full Business Case, about to be produced in phase 2.

Whilst the Strategic Business Case and Outline Business Case provided the direction for transformational change and described what the future could look like, the purpose of the Full Business Case is to justify the investment in transformational change, gain management commitment and secure funding.

Stage 2.13 consists of the following activities:

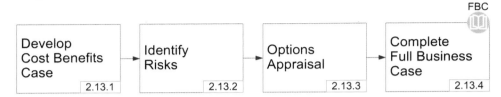

Figure II.2.15 – Activities in stage 2.13 – Develop the Full Business Case

2.13.1 Develop cost benefits case

The cost of transformation versus the value of having the Benefits should be reviewed now. These costs should include initial costs, programme costs, and on-going costs. The programme costs are based on the tranches within the programme plan that deliver individual Benefits or a group of Benefits. A year-by-year projection of costs needs to be calculated.

Similarly a year-by-year projection of Benefits should be calculated, showing the projected cash release or efficiency savings and/or the projected non-cashable Benefits.

A comparison of projected costs and Benefits can be balanced, where there is a mix of financial and non-financial Benefits, to give sufficient weight to the overall mix of Benefits.

The evaluation of the investment may result in revisiting either the Identified Benefits (stage 2.9) or the programme costing (stage 2.12).

2.13.2 Identify risks

The purpose of the Full Business Case is to provide a compelling argument that the transformation journey is worth proceeding with. The key factors affecting the decision will be:
- Benefits (from stage 2.9)
- Costs (from stage 2.12)
- Risks.

There are two questions that need to be asked about risks at this stage:
- **What are the risks of doing it?**
  Transformation is a radical change that potentially carries high risks to both the programme and service delivery. Risks need to be identified at this stage and assessed for likelihood and impact. Ways of mitigating each risk need to be defined. If the risks are unacceptable, this may result, for example, in changes to Benefits values, technology selection, programme structure, resource plan, phasing and so on.

PHASE 2 SUMMARY

This phase is used to plan and justify the journey to achieve the Vision. There are three main parts to this phase:

- Gaining a greater understanding of the solution by performing Logical Design and selecting products and suppliers
- Defining measurable Benefits
- Shaping the programme delivery, including the scope, plan timescales, risks and costs.

The Full Business Case justifies the proposed journey and, importantly, shows the Benefits that are to be gained directly against the costs that will be incurred.

Hints and tips

Look out for the some of the following aspects of phase 2 – Shaping and Planning.

Scope creep

Without a clearly defined idea of what you want to cover within the programme there is a risk of making the scope of the programme bigger than you had planned. A clear definition of what's in scope and what's out of scope provides a firm foundation for controlling the costs of the programme. The programme may gradually begin to drift away from its original objectives, timescales and budget so it is important to monitor the scope within all the phases.

Benefits

Benefits can be financial – cost savings or increased income, or non-financial – such as improvements in the quality of the service or product. It is important to consider the less tangible non-financial Benefits carefully. It may be that they make all the difference to customers, employees and the reputation of the organisation.

Whether they are financial or non-financial, it is necessary to measure the difference that the changes will make. This requires that the Benefits be accurately defined and a way of measuring the difference be found. Remember to measure how each aspect of the business is performing now so that it can be compared with the performance after transformation.

Risks of not doing it

It is worth asking the question what is the risk of not undertaking transformational change. What will maintaining the status quo mean for the business? Has less radical change been considered? Asking these questions may help to make a compelling argument for change.

Reflective questions

Reflective questions require you to examine your existing knowledge or experience before giving a thoughtful response.

This phase is used to plan and justify the journey to achieve the Vision. There are three main parts to this phase, Logical Design, Benefits identification and programme planning, all of which are key inputs to the Full Business Case (FBC).

1. Refer to stage 2.9. In order to identify Benefits you need to be able to define the things that will make a difference to your customers, employees and efficiency. What are the key points you need to get right if your organisation is to be successful? Examples might include speed of response, customer service levels, comprehensive product range, quality and financial strength. Add a measure. How will you know when you have made a difference – what difference will you have made?

2. Refer to stage 2.11. The programme structure and strategies that are agreed during this phase determine the path and approach for the programme. Map out (a) a programme organisation structure, and (b) the Benefits management strategy.

Phase 3 – Design

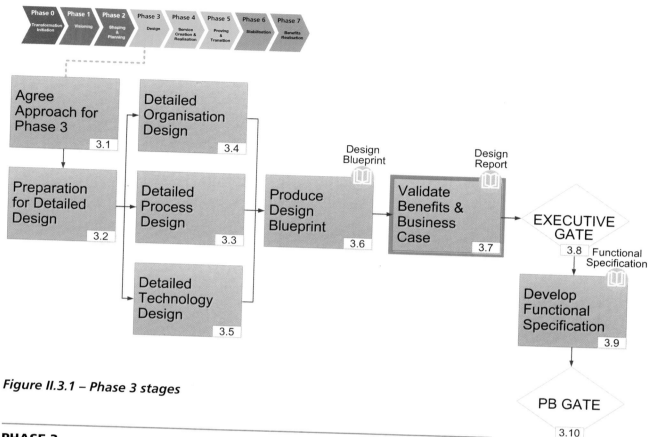

Figure II.3.1 – Phase 3 stages

PHASE 3

Now, the detailed design of the solution is carried out, defining how processes, organisation structures and technology fit together.

PURPOSE OF PHASE 3 – DESIGN

The Future Operating Model gave us the principles of the future operation, and Logical Design delivered a high-level view of the required processes, organisation and technology. This phase takes us to a detailed design of the solution that defines how the service will operate, including the flow of activities and information, who will perform them, and the tools and supporting systems involved.

The Full Business Case and Benefits will also be validated to ensure that they still stack up against the enhanced knowledge of the solution and how the solution will be delivered. Functional Specifications help to define in detail how the individual components will operate.

ROLES AND RESPONSIBILITIES

Programme Team – A wide variety of roles is required to facilitate process, organisation and technology design. The team will produce the Design Blueprint, Design Report and Functional Specifications.

Programme Board –The Programme Board will review the Design Report, the validated Full Business Case and approve the completion of the Functional Specifications.

Executive – The Executive approves the Design Report and any updates to Benefit Cards and the revised Full Business Case.

Programme Manager/s – The Programme Manager/s manage/s programme delivery and reviews the Phase Exit Criteria Checklist.

Benefit Owners – Benefit Owners sign validated Benefit Cards.

Benefits Realisation Board – Reviews any changes to Benefits and Benefits Realisation Plan.

Design Authorities – Process Design Authority, Organisation Design Authority and Technology Architecture Authority – Review relevant aspects of detailed design.

Quality Assurance Function – This group continues to advise and monitor quality and the use of CHAMPS2.

3.1 AGREE APPROACH FOR PHASE 3

Purpose

After the Future Operating Model delivered in phase 1, which formulated the principles of the future operation and the Logical Design delivered in phase 2, which provided the high-level design, phase 3 is concerned with the detailed design of the solution and how all the components fit together. It is important to take stock and review the path the programme will take through phase 3. The activities completed in this phase will depend on the nature of change. For example, if technology changes are envisaged, are any proofs of concepts required? Different paths may also need to be considered for different work streams working at a different pace.

Stage 3.1 consists of the following activities:

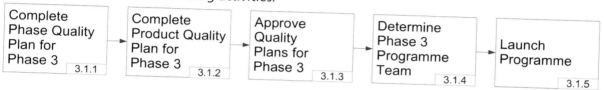

Figure II.3.2 – Activities in stage 3.1 – Agree approach for phase 3

3.1.1 – 3.1.3 Quality Plans

The approach is captured in two documents that are central to maintaining quality standards and managing client expectations:

- **Phase Quality Plan** – to tailor the stages and activities to the programme's needs
- **Product Quality Plan** – to ensure the quality of each product and how it is approved.

At the end of the phase, the **Phase 2 Exit Criteria Checklist** will be used to assess whether the phase objectives have been met. This document, therefore, forms a vital input into the development of Quality Plans and should be considered when they are being created. Lessons learnt from previous phases or other change initiatives should be considered when choosing the most appropriate approach.

These are key products from the Quality Management Framework, which is fully explained in section III.

3.1.4 Determine phase 3 Programme Team

Work carried out in phases 0 to 2 was carried out by a small 'pathfinder' team. With the scope of the programme approved, a larger Programme Team, which will start to design the solution in phase 3, can now be set up, with people identified, trained and brought on board.

CHAMPS2 distinguishes between the Programme Team who are responsible for delivery of the solution and people within the business who will ultimately implement the solution. The Programme Teams may include people from the business, as well as technical experts, consultants, business change managers, business analysts, communication specialists and project managers. Mobilisation should focus on getting people and resources in place, and this may mean pulling individuals out of their existing jobs, and finding office space and facilities. One of the first roles required within the Programme Team is the design team.

It is important that the Programme Teams develop objectives, roles and responsibilities and are inducted into the programme, the CHAMPS2 method and Quality Management Framework.

This is often an appropriate point at which to begin considering what type of communication and consultation will be helpful during this phase, in preparation for the activity in stage 3.8.

3.1.5 Launch programme

The launch of the programme is likely to involve two launch events, one for the Programme Team, including team members from the business areas, and one for stakeholders. The events should be lead by the Senior Responsible Owner and Programme Managers who need to explain the programme's objectives, structure and the Benefits. The approach to programme delivery, including use of CHAMPS2, should be explained and the plan outlined.

The Programme Team and stakeholders should also understand:
- What will make it successful?
- What is in it for them?
- What is expected of them?

The aim is to unite the Programme Team in a common purpose and also to gain commitment from stakeholders. Awareness of the Benefits and new ways of working is important and should form part of a wider communications exercise. It is also worth considering at this stage what messages will be communicated to customers of the transformational change.

3.2 PREPARATION FOR DETAILED DESIGN

Purpose
What needs to be done to prepare for Design?
Phase 3 – Design covers the completion of the detailed design that builds on the processes, organisation structure and technologies identified within Logical Design. Before the detailed design work can begin there are a number of essential activities that need to be done.

Stage 3.2 consists of the following activities:

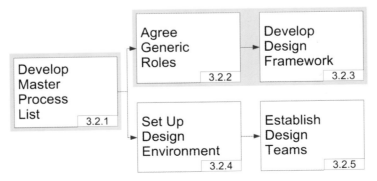

Figure II.3.3 – Activities in stage 3.2 – Preparation for detailed design

3.2.1 Develop master process list

The high-level processes were decomposed in Logical Design in stage 2.5. Now a full list of the lowest level processes needs to be created. The list is reviewed to work out which of these processes should be selected for detailed re-design. For example, a process which is fully automated or a process which is adopted unchanged, may not need to be designed.

This will produce a master list of processes to work from, including everything which needs to be reviewed, of which some will need to be re-designed.

Resist the temptation to design for rare events or exceptional circumstances in the first instance. Look at where the most value can be gained. It is also important to consider the complexity of the new processes, whether they are standard or non-standard, the Benefits to be gained and their impact on the business.

Standard processes may not need a formal workshop approach and may be produced directly into a process map format using the design team's expertise/experience of best practice. These 'standard' processes are then simply reviewed with the stakeholders and key members of the business team.

3.2.2 Agree generic roles

Before the detailed design sessions start, a master list of generic roles needs to be agreed. These are used within the process maps to determine which activities are to be performed by which roles.

Role titles, with descriptions, should be used consistently across all of the design teams. For example, if the role 'customer' is used by some teams and 'internal customer' used by other teams, designs will be ambiguous. Roles should also be kept at a generic level, in order to keep discussions away from specific jobs and responsibilities. At this stage the design only needs to distinguish between the 'plan', 'do' and 'control' types of roles.

3.2.3 Develop design framework

The design framework document for detailed design provides the necessary information for detailed design of high-level components identified during Logical Design and covers processes, organisation and technology. The document is particularly useful for participants in the process design workshops, to give them background and a common understanding of the requirements for process design before the workshop starts. It should cover:
- Any requirements specified in Logical Design
- The lowest level processes which have been decomposed in Logical Design
- The design principles
- The approach to be taken to the design, including the tools and techniques
- The products to be produced (also documented in Product Quality Plan).

The document should also include any information that could help, for example, any processes that work particularly well and should be kept or replicated, or any processes that should be avoided.

All of the design team members also need to understand the Benefit required to be driven from each process. This defines the level of ambition that needs to be satisfied through the design, such as simply 'fit for purpose' or best in class.

The organisation design section should list all the teams from the high-level organisation structures and provide detail on:
■ Team purpose
■ Key accountabilities
■ Key interfaces
■ Key measures.

It should also define to what extent the detailed design teams are empowered to make organisational changes and what consultations are required.

3.2.4 Set up design environment
The actual design tools and techniques needed by the team should be agreed to provide consistency and ensure that others within the team will be able to use and work with them. Typically, this involves configuring process tools, setting up specific graphics or templates and storage of maps. A repository for all documents should be held centrally.

The design environment should include access to the design tool for the team. Workshop locations will also be required which comfortably accommodate teams of five to 10 people, and should be stocked with appropriate equipment. Rooms that can be used throughout the detailed design stage are useful to allow the teams to maintain design wall charts, plans and so on.

3.2.5 Establish design teams
Process, organisation and technology design are performed in parallel by specialist design teams. The teams need to be trained in the concepts of detailed design:
■ The difference between Logical and detailed Design
■ The transition from Logical to detailed Design
■ Input into detailed design
■ Outputs of detailed design.

The process design teams will require specific training in:
■ Process maps design method
■ Generic roles
■ Process integration
■ Use of a process design tool.

All teams need to understand the links between process, organisation and technology, record the data relevant to other teams and involve or consult the members of other teams.

The teams also need to understand the way the design will be reviewed by three individuals or bodies: the Process Design Authority, the Organisation Design Authority and the Technology Architecture Authority.

3.3 DETAILED PROCESS DESIGN

Purpose

How will the new business operate?

Detailed process design continues where Logical Design left off. It takes the lowest levels of process decomposition and continues to break down the process into individual tasks. It will determine which roles and technology will be assigned to the tasks and for this reason it is helpful to document the process in 'swimlanes'.

This is typically done in workshops, and organisation and technology design teams should attend the process design sessions to ensure that the process design is achievable. At the same time they will collect requirements that process design poses on organisation and technology design.

Stage 3.3 consists of the following activities:

Figure II.3.4 – Activities in stage 3.3 – Detailed process design

3.3.1 Create process maps

For each process on the master process list a map is created, typically, in what is known as a 'swimlane' format.

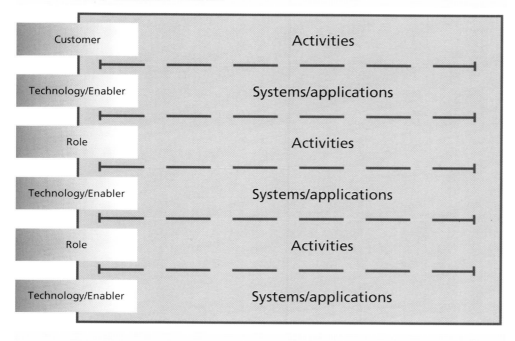

Figure II.3.5 – Outline swimlane process map

The process maps detail the sequence of activities within the process, which role carries them out and where technology is involved. It is advisable to document the detailed process map in swimlane format, one 'lane' per role.

In addition, the following information needs to be captured:
- Role details and any requirements for organisation design, such as separation of duties or specific competencies
- Activity descriptions and any requirements for future procedures
- Technology requirements
- Information flows and reporting requirements
- Data entities and data flows
- Interface requirements
- Development requirements.

Swimlanes
A process diagram that indicates which roles perform particular activities.

A simple example might look like this:

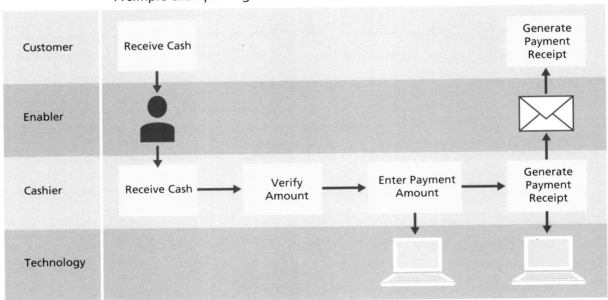

Figure II.3.6 – Example swimlane process map

3.3.2 Agree process variants

There will be a tendency to discuss and design a large number of variations on the standard process, and the business area is likely to come up with many reasons why all of these will be required within the new business.

Carefully consider whether processes are needed. For example, different service areas locations, or cultures might use processes differently. Alternatively, there may be slight variations based on financial thresholds, i.e. for transactions below a certain value one process may apply, whilst at another value a different process applies.

If there are variations it may be worth considering a family of processes with clear guidelines to determine which variant of the process to use in which circumstances.

Resist the temptation to design an unnecessarily large numbers of variants, and standardise processes where possible.

3.3.3 Produce process design documents

In transformation programmes covering a number of end-to-end business processes, a separate process design document is required for each end-to-end process, which is made up of several process maps. These are now amalgamated into a single design document, the process design document, representing the whole end-to-end process.

The document should include:
- Detailed process maps showing the sequence of activities, who does them and where technology is used
- Process variants
- Requirements on the organisation structure and technology arising from process design, such as automated workflows
- Process management and support required in the future.

This document should provide the Senior Responsible Owner and key stakeholders with enough information to walk through the end-to-end process. It also needs to provide the teams with sufficient detail to bring the design to life.

3.4 DETAILED ORGANISATION DESIGN
Purpose
How will the organisation be structured?
In this stage, the objective is to bring together the top-down team design from Logical Design (stage 2.5), and the bottom-up jobs and roles arising out of the newly designed processes. Jobs and roles need to fit into teams. This may require some compromise and changes to the organisation structure to create the optimum fit. For example, team and management structures may need to be adjusted to suit the new roles.

Stage 3.4 consists of the following activities:

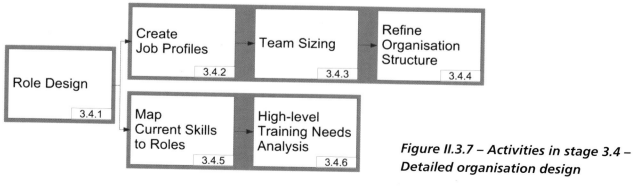

Figure II.3.7 – Activities in stage 3.4 – Detailed organisation design

3.4.1 Role design

The building blocks for our bottom-up organisation design are roles. Roles perform a sequence of activities mapped out in the new processes. These generic roles cover a number of processes and activities within processes. The roles are clustered and entered on to role cards and are then mapped to teams within the organisation structure agreed during Logical Design.

The team information is documented in the team definitions showing what each team and role is responsible for and who needs to approve it. It is also useful to be clear who has information and what they need to be consulted on and who needs to be informed about decisions or notified of the results.

A role card is created for each generic role detailing:
■ Key tasks performed by the role
■ Key relationships when performing the role
■ Separation of duties.

The role cards form the basis for defining job profiles.

The organisation structure should be updated showing the roles performed within each team. It is now a matter of identifying which of these roles could be performed by the same individual, so that we know which jobs need to be created and how many. This activity joins the bottom-up organisation design to the top-down organisation design.

Role
A set of responsibilities, activities and authorisations. A role may be undertaken by a number of different job-holders.

3.4.2 Create job profiles

The roles within the teams show which tasks will be performed in the team. In order to assign people to do the tasks, the jobs need to be defined. To do this the clustered roles documented on the role cards are put into logical groups that could be performed by one person and a job profile is created for each group.

A job profile details the duties the person will have including:
■ Core duties identified from role cards
■ Activities required of all employees of the business (such as training or personal development)
■ Management duties
■ Important tasks or projects not covered so far – in other words, out-of-scope processes
■ Other tasks that people have historically carried out.

The identification of additional duties may result in adjustments to the calculated team sizes. The jobs are then mapped to the organisation structure and the number of posts with the same job profile determined, using the team sizing information.

Job profiles form the basis for creating job descriptions within stage 4.4 – Develop organisation.

Job

A collection of functions, tasks, duties, and responsibilities assigned to one or more positions which require work of the same nature and level. A job holder may undertake a number of roles.

3.4.3 Team sizing

Once the roles have been mapped to teams, the team sizes can be calculated accurately. Team sizes were estimated during Logical Design, based on the Benefits case at that point. Several approaches can be used to size a team. The number of FTEs (full time equivalent) employees required could be determined from (in this order of priority):
- Existing baseline, with % process efficiency gain, or % volume change
- Existing baseline, with % estimated productivity improvement
- Last year's budget, with desired budget target reduction
- Current team size, with reduction negotiated with budget holder.

3.4.4 Refine organisation structure

A detailed organisation structure can be drawn, which covers the whole organisation from divisions, through the sections or departments, to teams and individual jobs. This is an opportunity to refine the structure and check spans of control, for example, how many layers there are in the hierarchy. Anomalies, such as one-to-one reporting or too many management layers need to be resolved. Revisions may result in adjustments to the previously calculated team sizes.

Once the organisation structure has been finalised, we can see how much the organisation needs to change. The new structure should be compared with the current organisation, to highlight the need for training, recruitment or redeployment.

3.4.5 Map current skills to roles

The purpose of this activity is to identify the existing staff within the affected business areas and map them all against the new job profiles and specific roles within those jobs. This is important in order to ensure that people are slotted into the organisation seamlessly and receive the right training, and that they can access the right parts of the new systems and receive appropriate communications. The mapping should encompass all members of staff. Even those whose jobs may not substantially change may require information about, for example, the changes or training in new technology.

What it does not do is define detailed job descriptions, person specifications, grades or terms and conditions. These will be fine-tuned in stage 4.4 when the organisation is developed.

The information will be used in the high-level training needs analysis (below) and the detailed design impact assessment which takes place in stage 3.6. In phases 4 and 5, it will be used, to populate jobs, schedule training and set up system access.

3.4.6 High-level training needs analysis

An appropriate training programme needs to be considered for the roles within the new organisation. This should follow the training strategy agreed in stage 2.11 when programme governance was developed.

First, a skills assessment is needed for the people mapped into new roles. The gap between current skills and the new skills required forms the basis for identifying training requirements. This is further developed into a course catalogue mapped to the roles to which the courses apply. All forms of training should be considered, such as classroom, workshops, e-learning, briefings and mentoring. It should also estimate of the cost of delivery.

The high-level training needs analysis will be developed further into a detailed training needs analysis within stage 4.4 when the organisation is developed.

3.5 DETAILED TECHNOLOGY DESIGN

Purpose

What does the technology need to do?

From the detailed process design, we know where the technology is going to be used and what for. We also know, from the organisation design, how many people will be using the technology. With this information it is possible to start to plan in greater detail. Technology design encompasses everything necessary to support the solution – from hardware to software, from paper forms to reports.

Stage 3.5 consists of the following activities:

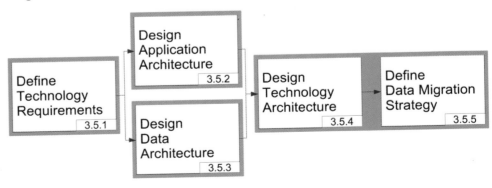

Figure II.3.8 – Activities in stage 3.5 – Detailed technology design

3.5.1 Define technology requirements

Before technology design work can begin, there should be a clear understanding of the technology requirements, so that the resulting design will support business processes and contribute towards strategic Outcomes. Some of the requirements will have already been identified at different stages of design and documented in relevant documents: the Future Operating Model, Logical Design and detailed process design. These will now need to be consolidated and any additional requirements identified.

In addition to functional requirements arising from business processes, all non-functional requirements should be identified as well, such as: system availability, security, audit requirements, data retention, scalability, supportability, disaster recovery and so on.

The choice of technologies should be in line with the organisation's overall information systems strategy and for this reason the requirements should be agreed with the Technology Architecture Authority. Technology design should also comply with relevant policies, standards and legislation, such as data protection.

3.5.2 Design application architecture

At this stage, the applications that are needed to support the business processes are defined, including:
- Which application systems are needed
- How they interact
- The relationship between processes and applications including workflows

The key applications will already have been identified in the earlier stages of design. Within this activity all applications that form the new solution are mapped, irrespective of whether they are existing applications or new ones to be developed or bought.

The applications should be described in terms of the capabilities they need to provide, rather than specifying the underlying technologies required at this early stage.

3.5.3 Define data architecture

In many instances data architecture will be included within the application systems. In other instances a data model will be developed first to drive the development of interfaces or bespoke applications.

Data architecture will build on information flows identified during Logical Design and detailed process design and will include:
- Definition of data entities, for example, customer, order or invoice
- Relationship between entities, such as one-to-one, one-to-many, many-to-many, generic–to-specific, whole-to-part
- Data management including database administration, data warehousing or data retention.

Data architecture should link back to business processes and provide a clear understanding of:

■ Where data entities are used within business processes
■ Where the data is created, transformed or transported, and reported.

The data architecture should also identify any data migration and data cleansing requirements.

3.5.4 Design technology architecture

The technology architecture defines the hardware and software that need to be in place to support the application architecture. It will typically be presented as series of diagrams showing:

■ Hardware and software infrastructure
■ Communications infrastructure, such as routers, switches, firewalls, and network links
■ Environments – for example, development, production
■ Physical location of servers
■ Mapping of applications onto the technology infrastructure.

A comprehensive list of technology requirements should be compiled with detailed specifications, for example, server specifications, data storage types, capacity, software releases. Technology architecture should be reviewed by the Technology Architecture Authority.

3.5.5 Define data migration strategy

The process of moving the old data into new structures needs to be defined. This involves examining current data, in terms of data structures, volumes, completeness and accuracy.

This will identify the source of the data and any conversion routines required. If, for example, the data is found to be incomplete or inaccurate it will need to be enhanced or cleansed.

The migration of data needs to be planned and this may involve freezing data for a time to ensure data integrity or using a phased approach for migrating large volumes of data. Depending on the completeness and accuracy of the source data, data enrichment and data cleansing routines or activities may be identified.

3.6 PRODUCE DESIGN BLUEPRINT
Purpose
What does the design look like?
During this stage, the three strands of design: process, organisation and technology, are consolidated into a single document, the Design Blueprint. This identifies all of the components, such as reports, procedures, jobs, etc. and shows how they work together. An impact assessment is also carried out and a change management approach outlined.

Stage 3.6 consists of the following activities:

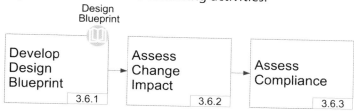

Figure II.3.9 – Activities in stage 3.6 – Produce Design Blueprint

3.6.1 Develop Design Blueprint

Progress through this phase provides greater and greater levels of understanding of the future operation. This information is brought together in the Design Blueprint. The Blueprint consists of a full list of components and how they fit together. This document is carried through into the next phase to allow the components that have been designed to be created.

Product title	Design Blueprint	Phase 3
Purpose	To document the detailed design to be used for the development of the solution	
Description	A document or set of documents describing in detail processes, organisation structure and technology and how all the components fit together	
Composition	■ Detailed process design, including process flow, roles involved and the use of technology within the process ■ Organisation design, including organisation structure, roles descriptions and job profiles ■ Technology design – identification of all components that need to be installed or developed and how they fit together ■ Information flow and data design ■ Policies, standards and procedures that need to be developed ■ Requirements for the development of the solution	
Input from	Future Operating Model, Logical Design	
Used as an input to	Functional Specifications, system test plans, integration test plans	
Approved by	Process Design Authority, Organisation Design Authority, Technology Architecture Authority	

Table II.3.1 – Design Blueprint composition

Design Blueprint

The Design Blueprint details the design of all the components that make up a solution and how they fit together.

3.6.2 Assess change impact

What is the impact of the completed detailed design on the business? By performing a full impact assessment the specific transitional activities are identified to prepare the business for the anticipated level of change, the technology to be used, how information will be managed and the behaviours that should be changed. As a result of this assessment, change management requirements will be identified, such as:

- Recruitment and/or redeployment requirements
- Training requirements
- Communication requirements around change
- Data preparation
- Transitional activities that are specifically required to prepare the business for the anticipated level of change.

Key stakeholders, including trade unions, may need to be involved at this point, reviewing the impact of organisational changes and new ways of working on employees.

3.6.3 Assess compliance

It is also important that the design complies with:

- Corporate strategies
- Legislation
- External policies.

Equality assessment is an important part of compliance assessment that helps to determine whether the new service meets the standard equality criteria in relation to race, disability, gender, faith, age and sexual orientation.

A formal equality impact/needs assessment (EINA) may be carried out at this point to ensure that the newly designed solution, including process, organisation and technology, is actually useable by customers or employees with a disability.

3.7 VALIDATE BENEFITS AND FULL BUSINESS CASE
Purpose
How accurate were the Benefits and the Full Business Case?
During this stage, all Benefits defined in phase 2 will be reviewed. This includes a review of existing Benefits and identification of new Benefits. Benefit Cards should be updated accordingly and set to status Validated.

Any changes to Benefits need to be reflected in the Full Business Case, which will then be resubmitted for approval. A summary of the Design Blueprint, together with the results of the change impact assessment and Benefits validation, should be compiled in the Design Report.

There is a chapter on Benefits Management in section III.

Stage 3.7.consists of the following activities:

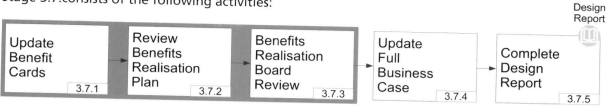

Figure II.3.10 – Activities in stage 3.7 – Validate Benefits and Full Business Case

3.7.1 Update Benefit Cards

Benefits were determined based on the anticipated performance. Detailed design shows whether the solution is likely to perform, underperform or exceed against expectations. To validate the Benefit Cards any changes to Benefits or new Benefits are identified. For example, during detailed organisation design a more efficient structure may have been proposed.

Benefit Cards should be reviewed and updated using the following criteria:
- Is the value of the Benefit likely to be the same?
- Is the baseline data still valid?
- Are the assumptions still correct?
- Are there any other business areas affected?
- What are the new timescales?
- Are there any new barriers to Benefits delivery?
- Are there any new dependencies?

In addition to changes there may be new Benefits identified. For example, during detailed organisation design a simpler organisation structure may have been proposed.

The Benefits value may need to be recalculated at this stage and the impact on the Full Business Case assessed.

The Benefit status should be changed to Validated and the Benefit Owners should re-sign the Benefit Cards. They should also enter the percentage confidence they now have in achieving the Benefit. Following the detailed design, which added another layer of understanding of the solution, there should be a greater level of confidence in Benefits realisation.

The updated Benefit Cards need to be reviewed by Benefits Realisation Board.

3.7.2 Review Benefits Realisation Plan

The Benefits Realisation Plan created within stage 2.12.4 can be revised in the light of changes or developed to a further level of detail.
- The expected values of Benefits and, consequently, the total value of the Benefits may have changed
- The projected timescales for Benefits realisation may have changed
- New Benefits may have been identified that now need to be included in the plan.

Activities already in the plan, such as the baseline data collection, monitoring and evaluation can now be planned to a greater level of detail.

The Benefits Realisation Plan will need to be reviewed by Benefits Realisation Board.

3.7.3 Benefits Realisation Board Review

The Benefits Realisation Board monitors whether the Benefits predicted are really likely to be delivered in the light of any recent changes. The Board reviewed Benefits in stage 2.9 when they were Identified and should now assess any changes to the Benefits. The Board will be interested in whether:
- All Benefits have been Validated
- The new Benefits values and timescales are realistic
- There is a commitment from the business to the Validated Benefits, with all Benefit Cards approved by Benefit Owners.

3.7.4 Update Full Business Case

The Full Business Case, initially produced during stage 2.13, now needs to be updated in light of the detail available from the overall design. This may include updates to:
- Service delivery
- Programme delivery
- Overlaps with other programmes
- Programme structure
- Governance and key strategies
- Programme plan and project plans
- Risks
- Benefits.

Based on any changes made, the programme cost needs to be recalculated. The business needs to answer questions like: 'Are the Benefits still worth the investment?', 'Are the overall Outcomes still achievable?', 'Are the programme and level of change still affordable?'.

The updated Full Business Case, together with validated Benefit Cards will be presented to the Executive during stage 3.8.

3.7.5 Complete Design Report

Design Report
The Design Report is a summary of the Design Blueprint aimed at senior stakeholders. It also explores how the completed design will affect the business.

The Design Report is an extract of the Design Blueprint, which provides an overview of the changes required to processes, organisation structure and technology. It also highlights the changes to Benefits and the impact of change on the business areas affected.

It is used together with validated Benefit Cards and the updated Full Business Case to gain approval from the Programme Board to proceed to the next phase of work: phase 4 – Service Creation and Realisation.

Product title	Design Report		Phase 3
Purpose	To provide the Programme Board with a summary of the design		
Description	The Design Report is an extract from the Design Blueprint suitable for a business audience. It also contains details of the impact of change and how the design supports the achievement of Benefits.		

Composition	■ Overview of design
	  - Process
	  - Organisation
	  - Technology
	■ Change impact assessment
	■ Benefits review		

Input from	Design Blueprint		
Used as an input to	Revised Full Business Case		
Approved by	Programme Board		

Table II.3.2 – Design Report composition

3.8 EXECUTIVE GATE

Purpose

Is the Full Business Case still valid?

Within this stage, the newly designed solution is submitted for approval. This should be in the form of the Design Report that contains a summary of process, organisation and technology design. Where changes have been made to the scope, Benefits, cost or timescales for the programme the impact these will have on the Full Business Case should be assessed. The proposed change management approach should also be reviewed. Any changes to the Full Business Case will need to be approved.

Stage 3.8 consists of the following activities:

Figure II.3.11 – Activities in stage 3.8 – Executive gate

3.8.1 Programme Board approval

In the first instance, the Programme Board needs to be satisfied with the results of the design, before the documents are submitted for Executive approval.

The Programme Board will review:
- The Design Report, which will give them an overview of the new ways of working
- The change impact of the new solution and the proposed change management activities
- Any changes to Benefits and Benefits realisation timescales
- Any changes to the Full Business Case.

Once the design has been approved by the Programme Board it needs to be submitted to other stakeholders for consultation.

3.8.2 Communication and consultation

Communication to stakeholders is important in all phases of CHAMPS2. This activity should focus on the latest decisions and developments that will affect them, as well as outlining the next steps to manage their expectations.

Key stakeholders may need to be fully consulted on the design and any changes affecting their business areas documented in the Design Report. They need to understand what the new processes will look like and what technology will be used. They should also be consulted on the initial transition and implementation approach. This early stage of consultation is central to ensuring buy-in to the new business processes and ways of working.

It is important to keep employees informed about any job changes, after the organisation design has been completed in this stage. Consultation may be required and include trade unions where appropriate. Representatives should receive an overview of new ways of working, anticipated job changes, skills required for the new jobs and the training that will be available to develop the required skills.

3.8.3 Executive approval

The Design Report and updated Full Business Case are submitted to the Executive for approval. If changes have been made to costs, Benefits or the overall scope of the programme then an Executive decision will be required to check that the programme remains viable.

The Executive needs to:
- Gain an overview of the solution and match it against the aspirations within the original Full Business Case
- Assess the on-going viability of the Full Business Case.

3.9 DEVELOP FUNCTIONAL SPECIFICATIONS

Purpose

What exactly does it look like?

The Design Blueprint identified all the components to be developed. Before development starts some of the components will need more detailed user requirements in the form of functional specifications. This will form the first

part of the specification process. There will be two levels of specifications:
■ Functional Specifications – how the component works from the users' point of view
■ Technical Specifications – how the component will be built.

Stage 3.9 consists of the following activities:

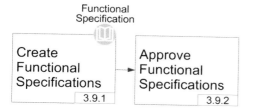

Figure II.3.12 – Activities in stage 3.9 – Develop Functional Specifications

3.9.1 Create Functional Specifications

Functional Specification
The Functional Specification describes how the components work from the user's point of view.

The Functional Specification is typically needed for technology components where there is a user interface, either for a customer or for a member of staff. For example, Functional Specifications may need to be created for:
■ New reports
■ Web pages
■ On-line forms
■ Back office applications
■ Data migration routines
■ Updates to legacy systems
■ Development of interfaces between new applications and legacy systems and so on.

The Functional Specifications should detail in non-technical language, what the system/s or third-party services need to do and how the component should operate under what circumstances. For example, where the relevant information comes from and goes to, what the navigation features are and the messages that will appear on a screen.

Product title	Functional Specification		Phase 3
Purpose	To describe how the component works from the user's perspective		
Description	The Functional Specification describes how the component works rather than how it is built. Each end-user technology component listed in the Design Blueprint, for example, on-line forms, reports, will be defined to the next level of detail in order to agree its functionality and operation within the relevant business area		

Composition	■ Purpose of the component and audience ■ Context ■ User operation ■ Look and feel ■ Data displayed/input
Input from	Design Blueprint
Used as an input to	Technical Specifications, unit test plans
Approved by	Business managers

Table II.3.3 – Functional Specification composition

3.9.2 Approve Functional Specifications

Once the Functional Specification documents have been written by the Programme Team, the content of each specification should be reviewed by the business. The purpose of this review is three-fold:

■ To ensure that the detailed specifications fully match the business requirements.
■ To bring the business up to speed. This knowledge transfer will provide them with an excellent background which they can use later during testing.
■ To gain approval from the business so that the Technical Specifications can be written and taken forward to the build stage.

It is important to get the Functional Specifications right, because once they are agreed and building starts, any additional changes to the systems/services will be time-consuming and, potentially, expensive.

3.10 PROGRAMME BOARD GATE

Purpose

Can we move on to the next phase?

During this stage, the phase 3 Exit Checklist and the Functional Specifications are reviewed by the Programme Board. Depending upon the result of this review, the programme will either be able to move forward into the next phase (phase 4 – Service Creation and Realisation), or the teams will need to re-visit the Functional Specifications and complete any gaps or issues identified.

Stage 3.10 consists of the following activities:

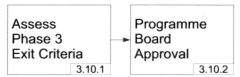

Figure II.3.13 – Activities in stage 3.10 – Programme Board gate

3.10.1 Assess Phase 3 Exit Criteria

At the end of the phase the Quality Assurance Function will perform an end-of-phase review of the programme using the Phase Exit Criteria Checklist. The Checklist describes the outcomes that are expected from the particular phase – irrespective of the actual approach or products. The criteria contained in all the Phase Exit Criteria Checklists are listed in appendix 2.

The checklist asks for evidence of how the programme has met each of the criteria. Against each of the criteria, the Quality Assurance Function, having reviewed the products and evidence, will record an overall quality assessment using a red/amber/green (RAG) method.

Once the Exit Criteria Checklist has been completed, the key learning points should be identified and made available to other programmes and projects in the form of lessons learnt.

3.10.2 Programme Board approval

The next step is for the Programme Board to review the exit readiness and the status of the Functional Specifications. They should make a decision on whether to proceed into phase 4 – Service Creation and Realisation, and to confirm that the design phase has been satisfactorily completed.

PHASE 3 SUMMARY

In this phase we completed the detailed design, which shows that all of the components fit together before any of the components are bought or developed.

Hints and tips

Design with purpose in mind

All of the design team members need to understand the Benefit required from each process. This will help to define the level of ambition that needs to be satisfied through the design: should it be simply fit for purpose or best in class?

Reflective questions

Reflective questions require you to examine your existing knowledge or experience before giving a thoughtful response.

1. Consider in what ways a product or service you know well could be affected by new ways of working.

2. Why is it important to have a Functional Specification before a Technical Specification and in what ways do you think they would feel like very different documents?

3. Map out the skills, expertise and experience in your business that could contribute to phase 3. What external skills and expertise would you seek to bring in?

4. CHAMPS2 asks us to define processes, organisation and technology. It is recommended that they be addressed in this order. Why this sequence and what are the arguments for and against starting with the technology options?

Phase 4 – Service Creation and Realisation

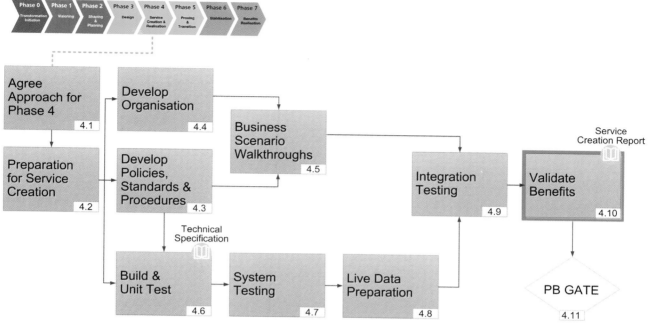

Figure II.4.1 – Phase 4 stages

Phase 4

In phase 4 the solution is developed and tested, based on the Design Blueprint.

PURPOSE OF PHASE 4 – SERVICE CREATION AND REALISATION

Phase 4 will produce the components identified in phase 3 and test the solution to ensure that it will work for its intended purpose, before it is handed over to the business to use.

The design developed in phase 3 is converted into:
- Components that support the new organisation structure, such as job descriptions or training courses
- Components that support the new processes, such as policies, standards and procedures
- New technology, such as application systems, interfaces and automated workflows.

Three stages of testing, unit, system and integration testing all are carried out to ensure that the solution will work. This phase culminates in the Service Creation Report, which concludes the completion of the solution.

ROLES AND RESPONSIBILITIES

Programme Team – Phase 4 requires specific and, in many cases, highly specialised skills to develop and test different aspects of the solution, such as procedures, training and technology components.

Programme Board – Approves the completion of the solution based on the Service Creation Report.

Test managers – Responsible for leading system and integration testing.

Test team – Performs system and integration testing of the whole solution.

Benefit Owners – Re-sign validated Benefit Cards.

Benefits Realisation Board – Reviews any changes to Benefits and Benefits Realisation Plan.

Design Authorities – Review relevant aspects of the Technical Specifications and any significant changes to process and organisation design.

Quality Assurance Function – Continues to advise and to monitor quality and the use of CHAMPS2.

4.1 AGREE APPROACH FOR PHASE 4
Purpose

In this stage, the team needs to review the path through the stages and agree the approach to take, using the Phase Quality Plan. It is important to ensure that appropriate skills are available in the Programme Team.

Stage 4.1 consists of the following activities:

Figure II.4.2 – Activities in stage 4.1 – Agree approach for phase 4

4.1.1 – 4.1.3 Quality Plans

The approach is captured in two documents that are central to maintaining quality standards and managing client expectations:

- **Phase Quality Plan** – To tailor the stages and activities to the programme's needs
- **Product Quality Plan** – To ensure the quality of each product and how each is approved.

At the end of the phase, the Phase 4 Exit Criteria Checklist is used to assess whether the phase objectives have been met. This document, therefore, forms a vital input into the development of Quality Plans and should be considered when the plans are being created. Lessons learnt from other change initiatives should be considered when choosing the most appropriate approach.

These are key products from the Quality Management Framework, which is fully explained in section III.

4.1.4 Determine phase 4 Programme Team

Phase 4 requires specific and, in many cases, highly specialised skills to create all aspects of the solution. This is likely to include specialists in relevant technologies, HR specialists to develop job descriptions and people specifications, training specialists to develop training courses, and people who will produce or amend Service Level Agreements, policies, standards and procedures.

This may include a proportion of representatives from business areas, required in particular for testing activities, which may enhance knowledge transfer.

4.2 PREPARATION FOR SERVICE CREATION
Purpose
What do we need to do to prepare?

Before all of the components are developed, the right environment needs to be in place and the strategies that affect the development process need to be clear, such as:

- Testing strategy
- Data cleansing strategy
- Training strategy.

These strategies will have either been created in stage 2.11 or existing organisational strategies may be used.

Stage 4.2 consists of the following activities:

Figure II.4.3 – Activities in stage 4.2 – Preparation for service creation

4.2.1 Set up development environment

There are a number of questions the development team should be asking, such as: do we want to develop solutions in a modular way, or focus on reusability? Is there a suggested sequence? What development tools and environments could we use and where shall we store solutions? When developing documents or software what are the most appropriate naming conventions and version control formats? Who will be responsible for each element of delivering the work?

The planning needs to cover:
- Development of policies, standards and procedures, where business owners of current documents may need to be identified and the rules of engagement clarified, the format agreed and appropriate templates developed
- Organisational development, including standards and templates for job descriptions and competencies, or the level of involvement from the human resources team
- Technology development, including what development tools need to be selected, the format of Technical Specifications or agreement on development principles. For example, is it better to create one specification per individual screen/transaction/whole application or to include all changes in one specification.

4.2.2 Review testing strategy

It is important that the Programme Team understands the approach to testing, documented within the testing strategy which has been developed in phase 2. Within phase 4 it is developed to a further level of detail.
The testing strategy is likely to cover:
- Scope and objectives of unit, system and integration testing in phase 4
- The method and tools to be used
- Additional types of testing, such as regression, stress or volume testing
- Tools used during testing.

The testing strategy also needs to include the management and reporting required and any escalation processes.

4.2.3 Review data migration strategy

New technology will inevitably mean that the data from legacy systems will need to be updated or cleansed and converted to the new formats. The data migration strategy will set the approach for both data cleansing and migration. The Programme Teams now need to understand the strategy and update it with more detail. This will help them to develop the necessary routines to ensure successful migration.

4.2.4 Review training strategy

Training principles are needed to ensure that everyone is working towards common standards for training development and delivery, as well as for detailed roles and responsibilities. In addition to end-user training, the training strategy should cover the training of support teams and testers for user acceptance testing and operational acceptance testing. Change control processes need to be agreed to manage changes to the training courses as development of the solution continues and components are still likely to change.

4.3 DEVELOP POLICIES, STANDARDS AND PROCEDURES
Purpose
How will the new processes work in the business?
Employees will need guidance through the new ways of working and new business processes in the form of policies, standards and procedures and service level agreements.

Stage 4.3 consists of the following activities:

Figure II.4.4 – Activities in stage 4.3 – Develop policies, standards and procedures

4.3.1 Develop policies and standards

Policies guide the decisions that are made across the organisation. They are supported by standards, which set the levels of performance required. In Logical Design and detailed design they were identified, but at that stage not written. Policies and standards should now be created or updated from the comprehensive list in the Design Blueprint.

Changes to policies and standards may need to be approved by leaders in the organisation.

4.3.2 Develop procedures

Procedures are a set of instructions that provide guidance on how a process or task is carried out. For example, these may include instructions on how absence is to be recorded on a new system or a complaint registered. These new or updated procedures, listed in the Design Blueprint, can now be created and agreed with business owners or representatives from the business area. These should be in a standard format so they are easy to follow and, once developed, will be tested in a business scenario walkthrough in stage 4.5.

4.3.3 Develop service level agreements

For the new business processes and organisational structures to work effectively, it may be necessary to agree a set of rules between different business areas, or between a business area and external suppliers. These would be documented in the service level agreements (SLAs). These ensure that the responsibilities of each party are clearly understood, the suppliers work to pre-defined and monitored targets and any issues are promptly resolved. It is particularly important to have service level agreements in place with any external service providers.

4.4 DEVELOP ORGANISATION

Purpose

What will people do?

The purpose of this stage is to develop details about the jobs in the new organisation structure, based on job profiles defined in organisational design in stage 3.4 and to develop the training courses that will be used to train individuals.

Stage 4.4 consists of the following activities:

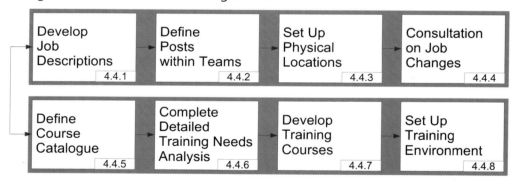

Figure II.4.5 – Activities in stage 4.4 – Develop organisation

4.4.1 Develop job descriptions

Using the job profiles created in stage 3.4, job descriptions need to be created. These should be generic and cover a number of jobs to enable greater flexibility and mobility of staff.

Job profiles are grouped by high-level duties and responsibilities and used either to update an existing, or create a new, job description. The job description should observe equal opportunities policies and include:
- Job purpose – for example, 'to provide', 'to undertake…'
- Duties and responsibilities – such as 'enter order details'
- Supervision given – who will supervise the job holder?

■ Supervision received – which jobs will be supervised by the job holder?

Each job description should have a defined set of competencies – the experience, skills, abilities, training, qualifications and other factors. This information is used as the criteria against which applicants are assessed.

It may be worth having the job descriptions and competencies evaluated by a job analyst. The job evaluation should be based on the organisation's grading structure. This determines the pay, rewards and terms and conditions for the job.

Job

A collection of functions, tasks, duties, and responsibilities assigned to one or more positions which require work of the same nature and level. A job holder may undertake a number of roles.

4.4.2 Define posts within teams

Generic job descriptions may be used in a range of areas of the business. The purpose of this activity is to define how many, and what specific, posts are needed in each team. So, for instance, the types of contract, working hours, start dates, aspects of the job specific to a particular business area and any security requirements, such as system or building access, should be established.

4.4.3 Set up physical locations

The new organisational structure including team sizes, roles, jobs and posts was designed in stage 3.4. The next questions to answer may include: 'where are they going to work?', 'what facilities are required?', and 'are there any opportunities for flexible or home working to reduce the space needed?'. The scope of this activity may vary, but could cover building new workspaces, creating floor plans and putting the infrastructure in place and planning to move into the new locations.

4.4.4 Consultation on job changes

Once the organisation details have been completed, the new organisation structure, job descriptions, grades, job volumes, job locations and any resulting changes need to be discussed in detail with key stakeholders, including trade unions, if appropriate. This should take place in accordance with any relevant human resources policies and legislation.

The impact on current staff needs to be assessed, along with the training and support that will be available to employees during transition.

4.4.5 Define course catalogue

New ways of working require appropriate training before the solution is implemented. A course catalogue may be set up to include external training and any training developed in-house.

The course catalogue needs to present an overview of the training required for each role, its content and structure, how it links to other training and how many people are likely to need to attend. All learning activities, such as classroom training courses, e-learning, mentoring or briefings should be defined and described in sufficient detail to enable planning of training sessions.

4.4.6 Complete detailed training needs analysis

A high-level training needs analysis was developed in stage 3.4. The content of training, the number of people to be trained and the requirements and arrangements for training venues administration and technology should be added. The primary aim of the training needs analysis is to confirm what training is needed based on the gaps between existing skills and the required skills for new processes. The analysis also determines what training methods to use to fit the culture and preferences of different audience types.

The detailed training needs analysis contains a course catalogue, a role-to-course map, tools for the development of training, tools for administration of training delivery, technical environment requirements, venue requirements and a high-level plan.

4.4.7 Develop training courses

Training can be in many forms and may be developed by a specialist team, purchased or tailored. The aim is to deliver the courses with a common look and feel, giving consistent messages and, above all, providing detail for users about the new processes and technology.

Developing training resources is, for some programmes, a significant piece of work and needs to be scheduled and planned at an early stage. The amount of development may vary, but is likely to include:
- Presentation, workbooks and worksheets
- Instructor notes
- Joining instructions, evaluations and administration materials.

4.4.8 Set up training environment

The purpose of this activity is to define the requirements for training venues, both in terms of type of venue and the length of time they are required.

Suitable training venues need to take into consideration types of rooms and layouts, how many people need to be trained, location, access to networks, use of equipment and so on. This may involve installation of hardware and software, setting up network access, loading appropriate data and setting up appropriate security profiles.

4.5 BUSINESS SCENARIO WALKTHROUGHS

Purpose

Will the new processes and organisation work together?

Business walkthroughs are one way to test the new processes and whether they are supported by the new organisation structure. The aim is to look at critical business scenarios that start and finish with the customer. The scenarios should be used to check the new processes and organisation structures step by step.

Stage 4.5 consists of the following activities:

Figure II.4.6 – Activities in stage 4.5 – Business scenario walkthroughs

4.5.1 Identify business scenarios

The walkthroughs need to be performed in a planned manner, using predefined business scenarios. The scenarios should cover high risk/high priority business processes, particularly scenarios that will occur frequently within the business, or will have a major impact on the business areas involved. They will also be used as a framework for the test scenarios in integration testing (stage 4.9).

4.5.2 Perform walkthroughs

These business walkthroughs aim to check that the processes will work and the jobs and roles in the organisation structure will be sufficient to support the processes. Policies, standards and procedures should be reviewed to see whether they support the new processes and whether the required business rules are covered.

Walkthroughs could take the form of facilitated 'table-top' testing discussions, with the business representatives asking questions like: 'Does anyone have it in their job description to handle this task?', 'Do you have enough information to do the task?', 'Is it clear where we hand over to another business area?', 'Are there any bottlenecks in the process?', 'What happens if something fails?'.

The results need to be fed back to the developers who may need to alter the sequence of tasks within processes, make changes to procedures to provide better guidance or make changes to job descriptions to incorporate additional responsibilities.

4.5.3 Sign off walkthroughs

The results of the walkthrough need to be signed off by business representatives and should be summarised in terms of:
- The number of scenarios successfully completed
- Coverage of the business areas by the scenarios tested
- Key issues identified and their impact.

4.6 BUILD AND UNIT TEST

Purpose

How do we create components that work?

The purpose of this stage is to build or configure the components according to the Technical Specifications produced. Each component should then be thoroughly tested as a unit, before system testing (stage 4.8). The objective is to test each component individually, including all business rules, validation, error conditions, data formats, etc, so that components are error free before they are entered into system testing.

Stage 4.6 consists of the following activities:

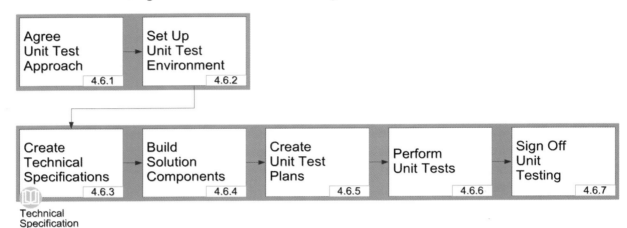

Figure II.4.7 – Activities in stage 4.6 – Build and unit test

4.6.1 Agree unit test approach

Development of individual components can be a fragmented process, and a common approach, based on the testing strategy created in phase 2, is needed to ensure the required quality of all products and that the appropriate level of testing takes place. Unit testing is normally completed by the team that has actually built or configured the solution/service and, in practice, takes place straight after the build. A degree of peer testing by another developer may be agreed within the approach.

The approach will also stipulate environments to be used, any tools or templates and the method of recording faults and reporting.

Acceptance criteria will be agreed that set the standard for unit testing, as well as exit criteria, that will determine whether unit testing is complete. For example, the acceptance criteria might include the level of defects within unit testing that is acceptable to the business (for example, can unit testing only be signed off if 100% of defects are fixed?).

4.6.2 Set up unit test environment

Before the designed solution can be built or configured and then tested the technical environments and infrastructure need to be created. The term 'environment' refers to the physical infrastructure, such as servers, software, databases and repositories as well as rooms, applications and tools. By this stage, a 'dummy' or 'sandbox' environment, where proof of concept/ prototyping has been undertaken, may already be in place.

4.6.3 Create Technical Specifications

The Design Blueprint describes the components and how they fit together. The Functional Specifications outlined how they will operate from the user perspective. The Technical Specifications show how the components operate internally, what they contain and how they are structured.

Technical Specifications should provide detail right down to report/screen/ form layouts, exact wording, data mapping, validation rules, use of different software components and settings and so on.

Some of these components may have been identified as a result of prototyping work during design. The Technical Specifications need to ensure that the functionality demonstrated can be successfully converted into a working solution and should be checked against the Functional Specification, developed in stage 3.9.

Product title	Technical Specification	Phase 4
Purpose	To describe how the component is built	
Description	The Technical Specification describes the internal structure of the component and the processing logic	
Composition	■ Functionality it needs to provide ■ Technical context ■ Internal design – composite parts and internal flows ■ Source and destination of data ■ Interfaces to other components	
Input from	Design Blueprint, Functional Specification	
Used as an input to	Development, unit test plans	
Approved by	Technology specialists	

Table II.4.1 – Technical Specification composition

4.6.4 Build solution components

This activity involves building or developing the technical components and any associated forms and then testing them. Building technical components involves everything from coding, developing and configuring to customising. It includes not only components that make up the solution, but also data migration, data cleansing routines and data extracts for Benefits evaluation.

The build is carried out by the development team and is typically an iterative process, with built or configured components being tested, amended or re-configured and then tested again by the same team.

It is important that the IT build is created using agreed software and coding conventions to ensure that systems work when linked together.

4.6.5 Create unit test plans

The test conditions will be identified within Functional and Technical Specifications. These need to be converted into exact test scripts. For example, recording down to the level of detail involved in entering invalid, past, future and current date to test the behaviour of the component in each situation and get all error messages.

If there are any changes to existing systems these need to be tested as well. Tests should include checking whether new changes have an impact on other parts of the system and that it will all still work.

Any data required to carry out the unit tests are loaded into the databases. Test data may need to be specifically created. The quantity of data may need to be low to allow data to be manipulated easily and should include both valid and invalid data, to ensure that tests will pick up errors.

4.6.6 Perform unit tests

For normal testing, the sequence followed should be:

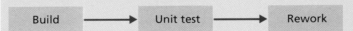

It is good practice to complete unit testing, using the test scripts, as near as possible to development – to ensure it is fresh in mind of developers. Any defects or incidents raised are recorded.

The results and the progress of any testing needs to be regularly reviewed, recorded and reported to the test manager. A summary or exit document covers whether the whole of the unit testing stage is accepted and agreement for any defect carry-over. If the unit testing exit document cannot be signed off, then the reasons for delay and/or defects should be resolved as a matter of urgency.

Ideally, every unit test should be completed before the next stage of testing starts.

4.6.7 Sign off unit testing

Once the entire unit testing has been completed a unit testing exit document should be produced and signed off by the Programme Manager. It should describe the:

- Test approach, acceptance and exit criteria
- Processes and supporting system/or service functionality tested
- Test results
- Results of defect resolution, including details of any defects that need to be carried over into the next stage of testing
- Readiness to move to the next stage of testing – system testing.

4.7 SYSTEM TESTING
Purpose
Does the system work?

System testing covers all the processes within a single system and tests whether they flow. Unlike unit testing, it does not focus on detailed operations such as testing the full variety of data or error conditions. It may include integration with other systems or other interfaces.

Stage 4.7 consists of the following activities:

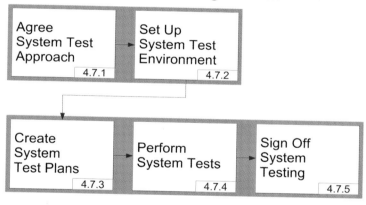

Figure II.4.8 – Activities in stage 4.7 – System testing

4.7.1 Agree system test approach

Before system testing can start, it is essential that the approach, based on the testing strategy from phase 2, is agreed with all system testing teams. This should include consideration of:

- Environments to be used
- Databases and refresh processes
- Any tools or templates
- Method of recording faults, their classification and prioritisation
- Approach to defect resolution, for example, immediate action by the author or bulk update at the end
- Reporting mechanism on progress and success of system testing.

In addition acceptance criteria should be agreed, to determine whether system testing is successful. Exit criteria are used to determine whether system testing is complete.

4.7.2 Set up system test environment

Typically, there will be a separate unit and system test environment. Any data required to run the system tests need to be loaded into relevant system test databases. The data could be a copy of the live data or specifically configured for the test. Either way, the data need to include both valid and invalid data, to ensure that tests will pick up errors and need to be of a sufficient quantity to allow all conditions to be fully tested.

Other preparation tasks include setting up system access, clearing down audit logs and preparing facilities such as printers and networks.

4.7.3 Create system test plans

Plans should be created to establish exactly what each system test will need to cover and which business components will need to be tested. The test should focus on the flow between components, rather than the detailed operation of components. The test conditions are identified from the Design Blueprint and Functional Specifications and should be organised into logical sequences, i.e. test cycles. An example of a test cycle could include ordering goods, paying for them and getting a confirmation of the order.

In addition to functionality it is important to prove that the system performs to acceptable levels and can withstand extreme conditions and this may include:
- Performance tests – evaluating the system's performance under normal conditions
- Stress tests – evaluating the performance of the system under abnormally heavy loads and identifying points when performance deteriorates or the system breaks
- Soak tests – evaluating the behaviour of the system over an extended period of time
- Regression test – proving that unchanged functionality still works.

The test manager needs to develop a detailed test schedule based on estimated test running times for each.

4.7.4 Perform system tests

For normal testing, the sequence followed will be:

System test → Rework → Unit test → System test

The system tests will either be satisfactorily completed, or a number of defects will be identified. These should be categorised based on severity so they can be prioritised. Once the defects are fixed the relevant component should be unit tested before the system test cycle is re-run.

4.7.5 Sign off system testing

Once all the system testing has been completed a system testing exit document is produced that describes:
- The test approach, acceptance and exit criteria
- The processes and supporting system/or service functionality tested within the system tests
- The test results
- Results of defect resolution, including details of any defects that will need to be carried over into the next stage of testing
- Readiness to move to the next stage of testing – integration testing.

The system testing exit document should cover whether the whole of the system testing stage is accepted and the requirement to carry any defects forward should be agreed with the Programme Board.

4.8 LIVE DATA PREPARATION

Purpose

How do we prepare for data migration and Benefits evaluation?

Whilst getting all the new components ready, the data is also being prepared for transition. The data will need to be:
- Cleansed and enriched to ensure accuracy for migration
- Captured to provide baseline information for Benefits evaluation.

Once the essential data preparation activities have been completed, a trial data migration run is performed.

Stage 4.8 consists of the following activities:

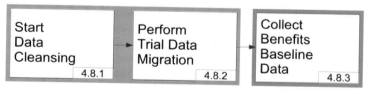

Figure II.4.9 – Activities in stage 4.8 – Live data preparation

4.8.1 Start data cleansing

The first strand of preparing data is to cleanse data sources to make them accurate, complete and suitable for automation. For example, it may be necessary to add post codes to records to support post code searches, change the format of information in the database, or remove or archive redundant fields or records. New, or enriched, data may also need to be added or derived from existing data by adding search criteria or reclassifying the data. Amending data sources is carried out by staff in the business, or can be automated.

4.8.2 Perform trial data migration

The second strand of data preparation is to prove, by testing with a trial run, that structures and volumes of data can be transferred successfully and will not cause the systems to run too slowly, or to identify where data needs further cleansing. This should also mean that accurate timings for the cutover of data can be established.

4.8.3 Collect Benefits baseline data

The third strand is that specific data needs to be collected to assist with the evaluation of Benefits. Data needs to be collected now to facilitate 'before and after' comparisons. For example, this could be achieved by collecting current data and performance metrics or performing customer surveys. The data is used once the solution is live to check that business Benefits have been Realised.

4.9 INTEGRATION TESTING

Purpose
Will integrated processes, organisation structures and technology work?
Integration testing means end-to-end testing of business processes by the Programme Team. It involves testing the whole operation, including job roles, support procedures, technology and processes, before it is handed over to the business in phase 5 – Proving and Transition. It is about testing realistic business lifecycles and includes all the new components, together with components that have not changed.

Stage 4.9 consists of the following activities:

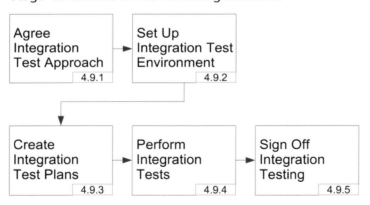

Figure II.4.10 – Activities in stage 4.9 – Integration testing

4.9.1 Agree integration test approach
Before integration testing can start, it is essential that the approach that will be taken is agreed. This will include consideration of the:
■ Approach to the development of business scenarios
■ Roles involved in the scenarios
■ Environments to be used
■ Databases and refresh processes
■ Any tools or templates
■ Methods of recording faults, their classification and prioritisation

■ Approach to defect resolution – for example, immediate action by the author or bulk update at the end
■ Reporting mechanism on progress and success of integration testing.

In addition, acceptance criteria is agreed, to determine whether integration testing is successful, and exit criteria devised, to determine whether integration testing is complete.

4.9.2 Set up integration test environment

The integration test environment needs to be set up and should mirror the future live environment as far as possible. Typically components should be loaded into the test environment, databases loaded with suitable data, system access set up and any specific facilities such as printers or networks prepared.

4.9.3 Create integration test plans

Business scenarios need to be identified that will test the end-to-end processes. For example, ordering goods: from placing the order and making a payment, through to delivery and return of faulty goods. These scenarios can be documented in the form of storyboards, rather than test scripts. The storyboards allow members of the testing team to use new procedures rather than following step-by-step instructions. The scenarios should test that the solution created is as described in the Logical Design and Design Blueprint.

A detailed test schedule should be produced based on the time taken to run the tests for each storyboard and scenario. Test managers should consider including trial data migration and cutover testing as part of system testing.

4.9.4 Perform integration tests

Once the test environment has been set up and the test plans are in place, the integration testing can start. The tests are performed according to the test plan, comprising a number of test cycles. Any defects will be recorded.

The information captured should include:
■ Date defect identified
■ Details of defect identified
■ Severity
■ Owner of defect resolution
■ Projected resolution date.

Typically, the defects would be fixed and retested in a unit testing environment, while integration testing continued. Severe defects may cause integration testing to stop until the defects are fixed.

A monitoring mechanism should be in place to record the progress on integration testing, the number of defects and any outstanding issues or workarounds.

4.9.5 Sign off integration testing

Once all the integration testing has been completed, an integration testing exit document is produced that describes:
■ The test approach, acceptance and exit criteria
■ The scenarios tested within the integration tests

■ The test results
■ Results of defect resolution, including details of any defects that will need to be carried over to phase 5 – Proving and Transition.

The integration testing exit document covers whether the whole of the integration testing stage is accepted and the requirement to carry any defects forward must be agreed with the Programme Board.

4.10 VALIDATE BENEFITS

Purpose

Have we built the right solution and are we still working towards the right Benefits?

At this point, it is important to take a step back to check the Benefits against what has been built and tested and to review the outcomes of phase 4. The status of the Benefit Cards remain Validated until the solution is fully implemented.

The Programme Board needs to approve the completion of the solution in the Service Creation Report.

Stage 4.10 consists of the following activities:

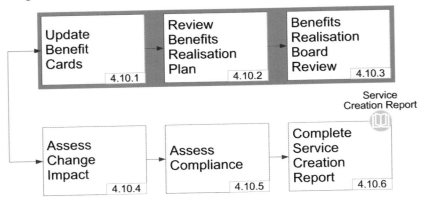

Figure II.4.11 – Activities in stage 4.10 – Validate Benefits

4.10.1 Update Benefit Cards

Two key things are required:
1. Review whether the Benefits Validated in stage 3.7 still stand.
2. Check that the components that have been built are likely to help deliver the Benefits.

This is the opportunity to return to the business to check that the solution built is what is wanted, that any changes are acceptable and that risks have been considered. This is the reality check before transition to the business happens. The temptation, having got so far, is to move on quickly. However, it is important to take this breathing space and assess the following issues.

■ How likely are we to realise Benefits as calculated on the Benefit Card?
■ If there are any defects carried over how do they affect Benefits?
■ Are there any new Benefits that require a new Benefit Card?

Even if the Benefit value remains the same, there may be a greater level of confidence in achieving the Benefit and, therefore, the percentage confidence on the Benefit Card should be updated accordingly. This is the third time that the Benefit Cards have been formally revisited (Benefits were Identified in phase 2 and Validated for the first time in phase 3). Benefit Cards need to be approved by the Benefit Owner for each updated business Benefit.

4.10.2 Review Benefits Realisation Plan

The Benefits Realisation Plan created within phase 2 – Shaping and Planning can be revised in the light of changes, or be developed to a further level of detail.

- The expected values of Benefits may have changed and, consequently, the total value of the Benefits
- The projected timescales for Benefits realisation may have changed
- New Benefits may have been identified that now need to be included in the plan.

Activities already in the plan, such as the baseline data collection, monitoring and evaluation can now be planned to a greater level of detail.

The Benefits Realisation Plan will need to be reviewed by the Benefits Realisation Board.

4.10.3 Benefits Realisation Board review

The Benefits Realisation Board monitors whether the Benefits predicted are really likely to be delivered in the light of any recent changes. The Board reviewed Benefits that were last Validated at the end of phase 3 – Design, and should now assess any changes to the Benefits. The Board will be interested in whether:

- All Benefits have been Validated
- The new Benefits values and timescales are realistic.

There is a commitment from the business to the Validated Benefits, with all Benefit Cards approved by Benefit Owners.

4.10.4 Assess change impact

Once the new ways of working have been fully tested by the Programme Team there is a greater level of understanding of the impact of the solution on the business areas. The changes may arise from, for example, new ways of working, complex new technology, new skill levels and culture change.

This assessment will enable us to plan transition activities within phase 5 to minimise any disruption and risk.

4.10.5 Assess compliance

During this activity the built and tested solution is again assessed to determine whether it is still compliant with:

■ Corporate strategies
■ External policies and legislation
■ Equality best practice.

An equality impact needs assessment may be required, particularly where changes have been made to the design of the solution. This will help to ensure that all elements meet the needs of different customer or user groups.

4.10.6 Complete Service Creation Report

The Service Creation Report communicates the status of the solution following unit, system and integration testing and any issues or outstanding actions. Some of the issues may be postponed or may result in de-scoping of the solution.

Product title	Service Creation Report	Phase 4
Purpose	To mark the completion of the solution by the Programme Team	
Description	A report produced at the end of phase 4, indicating the status of the solution after unit testing, system testing and integration testing	

Composition	■ Overall status of the solution
	  □ Process
	  □ Organisation
	  □ Technology
	■ List of components and their status
	■ Summary of unit testing results
	■ Summary of system testing results
	■ Summary of integration testing results
	■ Change impact assessment
	■ Benefits review
	■ Outstanding issues and actions	

Input from	Results of unit, system and integration testing	
Used as an input to	User acceptance testing, operational acceptance testing	
Approved by	Programme Board	

Table II.4.2 – Service Creation Report composition

4.11 PROGRAMME BOARD GATE

Purpose
Will the Programme Board approve?

The Programme Board needs to approve the completion of the solution and the Service Creation Report.

Stage 4.11 consists of the following activities:

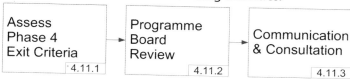

Figure II.4.12 – Activities in stage 4.11 – Programme Board gate

4.11.1 Assess Phase 4 Exit Criteria

At the end of the phase the Quality Assurance Function perform an end-of-phase review on the programme, using the Phase 4 Exit Criteria Checklist. The Checklist describes the outcomes that are expected from the particular phase – irrespective of the actual approach or products. The criteria contained in all the Phase Exit Criteria Checklists are listed in appendix 2.

The Checklist asks for evidence of how the programme has met each of the criteria. Against each of the criteria, the Quality Assurance Function, having reviewed the products and evidence, record an overall quality assessment using a red/amber/green (RAG) method.

Once the Exit Criteria Checklist has been completed, the key learning points should be identified and made available to other programmes and projects in the form of lessons learnt.

4.11.2 Programme Board Review

A shift of ownership of the programme is carried out in the next phase. The Programme Team will start to hand over ownership to the business areas. It is important that the Programme Board use this opportunity to ensure that the work of the Programme Teams is now complete and judged to be to the standard required for successful transition to the business. The Programme Board needs to assess the Service Creation Report and make a judgement on the overall status of the solution, check that testing has been effective and make decisions on whether any outstanding issues need to be resolved.

4.11.3 Communication and consultation

Communication to stakeholders is important in all phases of CHAMPS2. At the end of phase 4, key stakeholders, including staff and customers, should receive an overview of the completed solution and be consulted on the changes awaiting the business areas. Consultation with trade unions may also take place at this point.

The impact on staff will be much clearer at this point, including changes to processes, organisation design and technology. Communications should be carefully considered and planned, especially where there are likely to be changes in volumes of staff. Stakeholders should be given the opportunity to review the new job descriptions or changes to existing jobs, and what training is available to develop the skills required.

PHASE 4 SUMMARY

Phase 4 has produced the components identified in phase 3 – Design, and tested the solution to ensure that it is 'fit for purpose' before it is handed over to the business.

Hints and tips

Benefits and costs

At the end of this phase, the Full Business Case for the transformation may be reviewed to ensure that Benefits and costs are still on track.

Testing

There is a temptation to start system testing before unit testing finishes. It is important to ensure that components are effectively unit tested first. It will be a false economy if there are errors, and the testing will be invalid.

Rehearsal of technical cutover

The transition from existing to new systems and processes involves the co-ordination of a variety of complex and disparate tasks, normally within a short period of time, and with severe consequences if failure occurs. Rehearsals of technical cutover should be attempted where possible.

Reflective questions

Reflective questions require you to examine your existing knowledge or experience before giving a thoughtful response.

Phase 4 is concerned with taking the Design Blueprint and building and testing the new solution that can be implemented into the business in phase 5.

1. Refer to Stage 4.5 and 4.9. Consider some end-to-end scenarios based around your area of the business.
   - What different customer groups do you serve?
   - Can you think of any details that matter to your customer and should be tested during unit testing?
   - Can you think of any end-to-end scenarios involving your customer that could be tested during integration testing?

2. Unit and system testing are largely about ensuring that technology aspects of the new solution work. What additional elements of change are included in integration testing?

Phase 5 – Proving and Transition

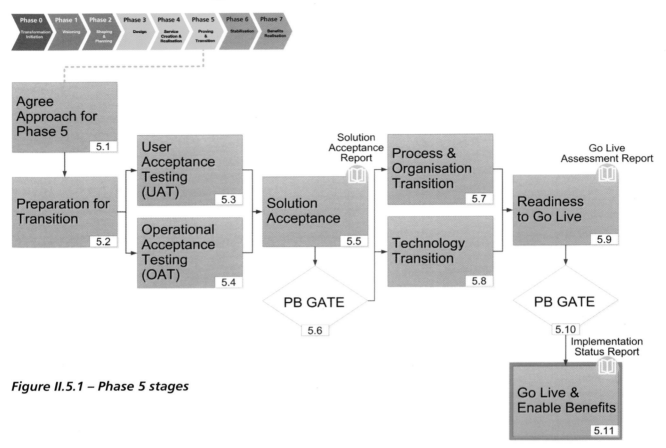

Figure II.5.1 – Phase 5 stages

Phase 5

In this phase, the solution is tested by the business, the business areas are prepared for change and at the end of the phase the solution is implemented into live operation.

PURPOSE OF PHASE 5 – PROVING AND TRANSITION

This phase contains two main strands of work that take the solution that was developed and tested in phase 4 and prepare the business to accept it and to go live.

The work will be carried out in two parts:

1. Transition – preparing the business for the new solution including comprehensive user and operational acceptance testing to ensure that the business areas are ready when the solution is implemented.

2. Implementation or Go-live – actively moving to the new ways of working.

At the beginning of phase 5 the ownership of the solution shifts from the Programme Team to the business.

ROLES AND RESPONSIBILITIES

Programme Team – The initial development team will support UAT, transition and implementation of the solution. New roles will be introduced from the business.

Programme Board – Approves the Solution Acceptance Report and Go-live Assessment.

Business support team – A temporary business support team is set up to provide front line support to end-users during UAT in phase 5 and Stabilisation in phase 6.

UAT and OAT teams – Perform end-to-end testing to ensure that the solution and support processes work.

Benefit Owners – Sign Enabled Benefits

Benefits Realisation Board – To be informed when Benefits are enabled and whether Benefits Realisation is likely to happen as planned.

Quality Assurance Function – This group continues to provide advice and to monitor quality and the use of CHAMPS2.

5.1 AGREE APPROACH FOR PHASE 5

Purpose

It is important to review the path taken at the beginning of each phase to ensure that the activities are relevant and support development of the best solution. The composition of the phase 5 team also needs to be determined to ensure that it meets implementation and support requirements.

Stage 5.1 consists of the following activities:

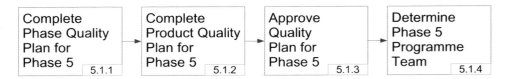

Figure II.5.2 – Activities in stage 5.1 – Agree approach for phase 5

5.1.1 – 5.1.3 Quality Plans

The approach is captured in two documents that are central to maintaining quality standards and managing client expectations:

- **Phase Quality Plan** – to tailor the stages and activities to the programme's needs
- **Product Quality Plan** – to ensure the quality of each product and how each is approved.

At the end of the phase the **Phase 5 Exit Criteria Checklist** should be used to assess whether the phase objectives have been met. This document, therefore, forms a vital input into the development of Quality Plans and should be considered when they are being created. Lessons learnt from other change initiatives should be considered when choosing the most appropriate approach.

These are key products from the Quality Management Framework, which is fully explained in section III.

5.1.4 Determine phase 5 Programme Team

Phase 5 requires a number of new and different streams of work to be created, led by the implementation manager and comprising:
- User acceptance testing test manager
- Operational acceptance testing test manager
- Change managers from individual business areas
- Training manager
- Business support manager
- Technical managers from specialist technology teams
- Implementation manager.

These managers create their own delivery teams and create an overall plan that will form the basis for detailed planning within their team.

This is often an appropriate point at which to begin considering what type and level of communication and consultation will be helpful during this phase, in preparation for the activities within stage 5.7.

5.2 PREPARATION FOR TRANSITION

Purpose

What can we do to ensure a smooth transition to the new organisation?

Key elements of the work that need to be completed within phase 5 are the transition and implementation of the new processes, organisation structure and technology. In this stage, the focus is on ensuring that these activities are supported by:

- An overall plan that forms the basis for detailed planning within individual teams
- Clear Go-live criteria that will focus the teams' effort towards successful implementation.

Stage 5.2 consists of the following activities:

Figure II.5.3 – Activities in stage 5.2 – Preparation for transition

5.2.1 Develop overall transition plan

Plans to support transition should be based on the change management strategy developed in stage 2.11. A high-level plan should be developed for the transition period. This should include:

- User acceptance testing
- Operational acceptance testing
- Transition and implementation within business areas
- Transition and implementation of technology.

It is vital to consider any key dependencies within the plan. For example, between recruitment and training or between software installation and data migration. The overall plan forms the basis for detailed planning in individual teams.

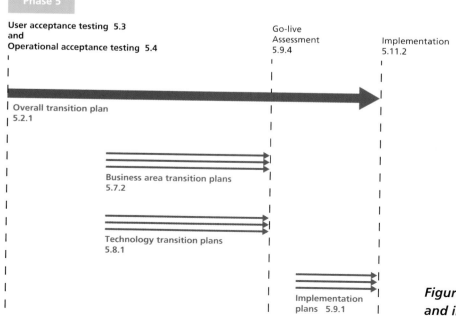

Figure II.5.4 – Example transition and implementation plans

5.2.2 Establish business support

Before the solution is handed over to the business either for testing or live operation, a support mechanism needs to be put in place to resolve end-user queries and manage any fixes or enhancements.

A temporary stabilisation support team, made up of members of the Programme Team, will be set up to provide help in the resolution of issues arising during:
- User acceptance testing
- Operational acceptance testing
- Training
- Transition
- Implementation and post implementation.

It will be in operation until the solution is fully stabilised at the end of phase 6 – Stabilisation. The transition of support to the business as usual support team should be planned from the outset, including knowledge transfer and the handover process.

The business support team deals with both business process queries and technical issues. The support processes developed as part of the solution should now be put in place, the relevant tools installed and the team trained.

5.2.3 Define Go-live criteria

All activities within phase 5 are designed to achieve the common goal of a successful implementation of the solution into live operation. Go-live criteria provide a checklist to assess whether the solution and business are ready, and form the basis for assessing the readiness for implementation in stage 5.9.4. The criteria could, for example, include:
- User acceptance testing and operational acceptance testing complete and all issues resolved or workarounds agreed
- Support team in place and fully trained
- System accesses arranged
- People who need to use the system trained to an acceptable level
- Data cleansing completed
- Jobs fully populated
- Workplaces ready
- Infrastructure set up
- Hardware and software installed
- User profiles and security accesses set up.

Go-live criteria should have an assigned owner with responsibility for delivering the solution. The criteria should encompass all business areas involved and cover all specialist areas, such as technology.

Go-live criteria will be used to judge whether the solution is fit for implementation and business areas are prepared.

This example shows the role of go-live criteria in the assessment of readiness for implementation.

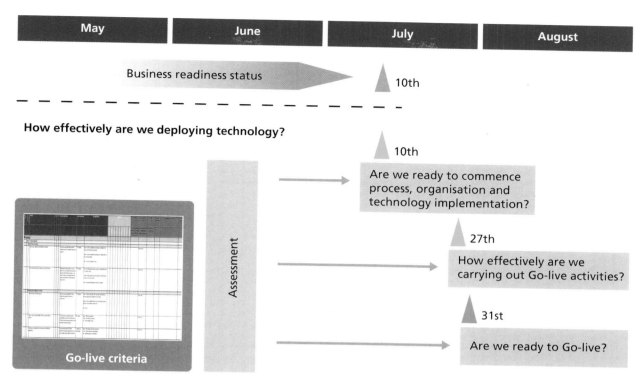

Figure II.5.5 – Example Go-live readiness assessment against criteria

5.3 USER ACCEPTANCE TESTING (UAT)

Purpose

Does the solution meet the requirements of the business?

User acceptance testing should be used to prove that the whole solution meets all business requirements. Tests will be based on business scenarios reflecting end-to-end business processes, not just technology components. They should be performed by testers, with minimum input from the Programme Team. The testers should be fully trained and during testing will rely on standard documentation such as training manuals, policies, standards and procedures. A stabilisation business support team should be in place to manage any defects or problems encountered.

Stage 5.3 consists of the following activities:

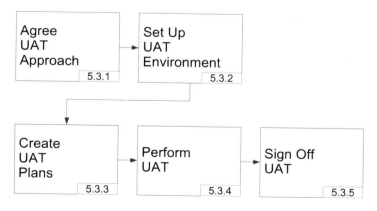

Figure II.5.6 – Activities in stage 5.3 – User acceptance testing

5.3.1 Agree UAT approach

Before user acceptance testing can start, it is essential that the approach to be taken is agreed. This includes consideration of:

- How will business scenarios be developed?
- Which roles are involved in the scenarios?
- What environments will be used?
- What databases and refresh processes are required?
- Are any tools or templates required?
- What support mechanisms will need to be agreed with the stabilisation support group; who will be logging any defects and managing defect resolution?
- How will we report progress on UAT?

In addition, acceptance criteria should be agreed to determine whether UAT is successful, and exit criteria to determine whether UAT is complete.

5.3.2 Set up UAT environment

The test environment needs to be set up to mirror the future live environment as far as possible. Preparation tasks include:

- Loading components into the UAT environment
- Loading databases with suitable data, typically an extract of live data
- Settin up system access for testers.

Sufficient thought needs to be given to test locations:

- Is the testing to take place in one or multiple locations?
- How large will each testing team be?
- For what period will locations need to be available?
- What infrastructure access, such as access to the internet, is required?
- What facilities are required within each testing room, to allow each test to be done? For example: phones, desks, flipcharts, screens
- Between what hours will testing be done and will 'out of normal hours' access be required?

5.3.3 Create UAT plans

User acceptance testing focuses on end-to-end and realistic business processes, such as testing whether, when a customer requests a service, they receive it, and all aspects of the process are run efficiently. Suitable business scenarios need to be identified. These are then developed into storyboards rather than detailed test scripts. Members of the test team are required to carry out the process, using new procedures and/or training manuals, rather than following step-by-step instructions.

To test the new organisation structure, team members are allocated roles within the new processes and appropriate training should be provided.

The test scenarios can then be sequenced into a test schedule. Typically, the test schedule is organised into test cycles reflecting the business processing cycles.

5.3.4 Perform UAT

Once the test environment has been set up and the test plans are in place, the user acceptance testing can begin. The tests should be performed according to the test schedule, comprising a number of test cycles.

Any defects should be logged by the support team and either immediately resolved or passed on to the Programme Team for resolution or a workaround. Typically, the defects would be fixed and retested in the unit testing environment, while UAT continues. Severe defects may cause UAT to stop until the defects are fixed.

A monitoring mechanism should be in place to record progress on UAT, including the number of defects and any outstanding issues or workarounds.

5.3.5 Sign off UAT

Once all the user acceptance tests have been completed a UAT exit document is produced that describes:
- The test approach, acceptance and exit criteria
- The scenarios tested within UAT
- The test results
- Results of defect resolution
- Any outstanding defects and planned actions.

The UAT results should be discussed with relevant business areas and the impact of any outstanding issues assessed. The completion of UAT is signed off by the UAT test manager.

5.4 OPERATIONAL ACCEPTANCE TESTING (OAT)

Purpose

Is the appropriate support for new technology, roles and ways of working in place?

Operational acceptance testing (OAT) is an independent test activity which can run in parallel to user acceptance testing. The purpose of OAT is to prove that the solution can be successfully supported once it goes live and will achieve expected performance levels.

Stage 5.4 consists of the following activities:

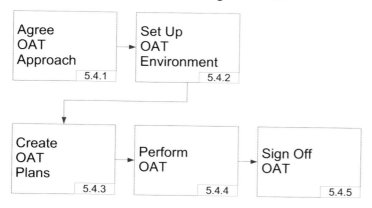

Figure II.5.7 – Activities in stage 5.4 – Operational acceptance testing

5.4.1 Agree OAT approach

Before OAT can start, it is essential that the approach is agreed. This includes considering the following:
- How will operational scenarios be developed?
- Which roles are involved in the scenarios
- What environments will be used?

- What databases and refresh processes are required?
- Are any tools or templates required?
- What support mechanisms will need to be agreed with the Programme Team?
- How will we report progress on OAT?

In addition, the acceptance and exit criteria should be agreed. They will be used to determine whether OAT is successful, and to determine whether OAT is complete.

Once the approach has been agreed, the OAT team should be identified and trained.

Depending on what role is assigned, the training should cover:
- New systems and their expected performance in terms of response times, availability and resilience
- Any service level agreements (SLAs) they need to test against
- Support processes and support tools.

5.4.2 Set up OAT environment

Before OAT can begin, the test environment needs to be set up. This needs to mirror the future live environment as far as possible. For example, a separate environment might need to be set up, a future live environment might be used or the environment might be shared with UAT, assuming any scheduling overlaps are resolved.

Preparation tasks include:
- Hardware/software installation
- Loading databases with suitable data
- Installation of support tools
- Setting up system access for testers.

The OAT team is likely to be comparatively small. Nevertheless, thought needs to be given to test locations, and facilities required, as well as the period of availability and any out-of-hours' access.

5.4.3 Create OAT plans

Operational acceptance testing focuses on support processes and therefore has to be based on realistic support scenarios, representing a variety of queries, support requests, failures or performance issues.

Suitable operational scenarios need to be identified, which are then developed into storyboards, describing the symptoms and underlying reasons for the problem, rather than how they are resolved. This requires members of the testing team to use the tools available and apply the new support procedures, rather than following test scripts.

Testing should cover:
- Business process and technology support
- Differing severity of issues from queries to system failures
- All roles involved, from frontline call handling to specialist teams.

The test scenarios can then be sequenced into a test schedule. Typically, the test schedule is organised into test cycles reflecting the support process cycles.

5.4.4 Perform OAT
The tests will be performed and any defects should be recorded and either resolved by specialist teams or a temporary workaround may be found. Typically, the defects would be fixed and retested in the unit testing environment, while OAT continues. Severe defects may cause OAT to stop until the defects are fixed.

A monitoring mechanism should be in place to record progress on OAT, including the number of defects and any outstanding issues or workarounds.

5.4.5 Sign off OAT
Once all the operational acceptance tests have been completed, an OAT exit document is produced that describes:
■ The test approach, acceptance and exit criteria
■ The scenarios tested within the OAT
■ The test results
■ Results of defect resolution
■ Any outstanding defects and planned actions.

The OAT results should be discussed with the business areas affected and, if necessary, with the Technology Architecture Authority. The completion of OAT should be signed off by the OAT manager.

5.5 SOLUTION ACCEPTANCE
Purpose
Is the solution fully functional and does it meet business requirements?
The business should now have a clearer picture about the overall state of the solution. This includes whether the new processes meet business requirements, whether all components are fully operational and any outstanding issues. The findings are documented in the Solution Acceptance Report.

Stage 5.5 consists of the following activity:

Figure II.5.8 – Activity in stage 5.5 – Solution acceptance

5.5.1 Produce Solution Acceptance Report

At the end of the UAT and OAT we are ready to report on whether the business considers the solution is fit for purpose.

Product title	Solution Acceptance Report	Phase 5
Purpose	To assess whether the solution is fit for purpose in the business	
Description	This report is based on the results of User Acceptance Testing and Operational Acceptance Testing. Testing should have proved that the solution works in real business situations and that the support processes work as well	
Composition	■ Overall status of the solution ■ List of components and their status ■ Summary of user acceptance testing results ■ Summary of operational acceptance testing results ■ Outstanding issues and actions	
Input from	Results of User Acceptance Testing and Operational Acceptance Testing	
Used as an input to	Go-live Assessment	
Approved by	Programme Board	

Table II.5.1 – Solution Acceptance Report composition

If there are any outstanding issues, the report should explain the:
■ Severity – can we implement without them?
■ Complexity and the effort needed to resolve them
■ Impact on Benefits realisation – for example, will the issues reduce Benefits?
■ Workaround options.

The report is submitted to the Programme Board to formally accept the solution.

5.6 PROGRAMME BOARD GATE

Purpose

Is the solution acceptable?

This gate is used to formally approve the solution by the Programme Board, following the completion of user acceptance testing and operational acceptance testing, and an assessment of any outstanding issues. The Programme Board will receive the Solution Acceptance Report summarising the state of the solution and outstanding issues and their impact.

Stage 5.6 consists of the following activity:

Figure II.5.9 – Activity in stage 5.6 – Programme Board gate

5.6.1 Programme Board review

The Programme Board reviews the Solution Acceptance Report to see whether:
- User Acceptance Testing and Operational Acceptance Testing have been performed to the required standard
- The solution is fit for purpose and can be implemented once the business areas are ready
- There are acceptable operational and support processes in place.

The decision has to be made whether issues need to be resolved before going live and therefore need to be included in the Go-live criteria, or whether they can wait until after implementation.

5.7 PROCESS AND ORGANISATION TRANSITION
Purpose
How shall we prepare business areas for change?
A key element of the work that needs to be completed within phase 5 is the implementation of the new organisation structure and the new ways of working. This is typically managed within individual business areas lead by business implementation managers and business change managers.

At the end of this stage the business areas should be ready to go live and adopt the new ways of working.

Stage 5.7 consists of the following activities:

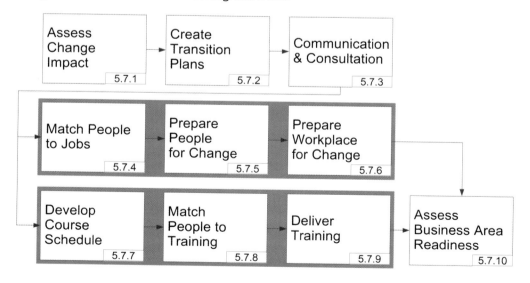

Figure II.5.10 – Activities in stage 5.7 – Process and organisation transition

5.7.1 Assess change impact

A detailed impact analysis of the new business solution within individual business areas should be carried out. This is led by the business change manager who reviews the magnitude, and the types, of changes facing the business area and plans appropriate activities to ensure that changes go ahead. To realise Benefits successfully a business area may, for example, need to get people in the business prepared for:

- Changes to the organisation structure
- Changes to processes
- Unfamiliar terminology
- New technology
- Changes to the work environment
- New culture.

5.7.2 Create transition plans

A detailed transition plan should be created within each business area to prepare for change and minimise risks and disruption. Each business area plan needs to be aligned with the overall transition plan and should take into account any dependencies on different programmes or business areas. For example, there may be a dependency on technology being ready. Transition plans typically cover:

- Matching people to jobs
- Recruitment or redeployment
- Training
- Making support arrangements
- Publishing new procedures
- Office moves
- Setting up infrastructure, for example, printers, scanners and telephones.

5.7.3 Communication and consultation

Communication around this time is essential if the new solution and ways of working are to be successfully implemented into the business areas. It is essential that the business areas fully understand what is going to be happening during the transition stage and what is going to be expected of them during this time.

At the same time, external communication is needed to inform customers and other contacts about changes that affect them and the timetable of events. Communication planning should involve:

- An analysis of the range of audiences who need to be informed
- Formulating key messages
- Identifying communication channels
- Defining appropriate communication events.

Once the change impact has been assessed and transition plans created, a period of consultation may be required. This will vary from organisation to organisation and may include for example:

- Consultation with customers, employees and interested parties
- Consultation with stakeholders
- Consultation with trade unions.

5.7.4 Match people to jobs

The aim is to select people from the current organisation for the new/ updated posts identified in stage 4.4. There are many different ways that staff can be assimilated into a new organisation structure. For example:

- Skills/competencies matching – a person's competencies are matched against the job description and person specification
- Job matching – if there is a direct correlation between the person's old post and the new one proposed
- Grade matching – a direct 'slotting' of individuals who are of the same grade or level
- Performance criteria – if there are several employees who match the criteria, selection may be made on past performance.

If there is no suitable match for a job among existing staff, the post may be filled by internal or external recruitment. On the other hand, there might be people within the business area who no longer fit into the new organisation and need to be re-deployed.

5.7.5 Prepare people for change

People within affected business areas need to understand and prepare for the upcoming transformational change. It is important to emphasise:

- The advantages to them and the organisation
- The impact on them and their immediate team
- Their new responsibilities and expected behaviours
- Participation in training
- Support available to get them through change
- The opportunities for personal development
- The timetable of events.

Once job changes have been decided, communication is needed to address individual personal concerns and identify any personal training needs. For example, there might be a requirement for training in basic computer skills as a prerequisite to the main training programme, or individuals may find management coaching helpful.

5.7.6 Prepare workplace for change

Any changes to the work environment need to be ready before the solution goes live and should be planned through the transition period. For example, we may need to:

- Design new office layouts
- Refurbish offices
- Set up infrastructure, such as networks
- Install printers and phones
- Make arrangements for security access
- Plan office moves.

5.7.7 Develop course schedule

The course schedule lists all training events and when and where they are happening. For classroom based courses, a trainer should be assigned to each event at this point.

The course schedule should be built from the information contained within the course catalogue defined in stage 4.4, which should include the length of the course, number of participants per session and total number of staff to be trained.

Different views of the course schedule may be required which show the training planned for individual business areas, or courses facilitated by specific trainers or room utilisation.

5.7.8 Match people to training

Once the training schedule has been produced the business areas need to ensure that appropriate staff are selected for the training available. The potential participants from each business area have been identified during role mapping and skills assessment exercise within phase 3 – Design. Within this activity the lists are finalised, based on the input from the selection and recruitment process and individual training needs.

The lists show which roles each person performs. People's roles can then be matched to training courses within the course catalogue. A trainee-to-course list is produced that forms the basis for sending the invitations to the business areas and booking the courses.

Participants may require joining instructions and a course outline explaining the course aims and objectives, as well as brief content and any prerequisites to the course. Reminders may need to be sent to the participants before the course to maximise attendance.

5.7.9 Deliver training

Training could have a major influence on how the transformational changes are accepted by the business areas and it needs to be right first time. It could take many forms, which may or may not involve the Programme Team.

Pre-course checklists should be prepared and reviews of the training environment should be carried out. Training delivery needs to be of a consistently high standard and evaluated by participants to identify any potential improvements or lessons learnt.

Ensuring that sufficient knowledge and understanding of the processes and application systems to be able to perform their future roles is vital. This may involve using an online assessment tool, or can be done manually where the trainer undertakes the assessment.

5.10 PROGRAMME BOARD GATE
Purpose
Are we ready to go live?
This stage is the last Programme Board gate before the solution goes live. The purpose of this gate is to confirm that the implementation of the new solution can go ahead and that the Go-live Criteria have been met.

Stage 5.10 consists of the following activities:

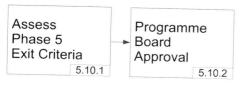

Figure II.5.13 – Activities in stage 5.10 – Programme Board gate

5.10.1 Assess Phase 5 Exit Criteria
At the end of the phase, the Quality Assurance Function performs an end-of-phase review on the programme using the Phase 5 Exit Criteria Checklist. The Checklist describes the outcomes that are expected from this particular phase – irrespective of the actual approach or products. The criteria contained in all the Phase Exit Criteria Checklists are listed in appendix 2.

The Checklist asks for evidence of how the programme has met each of the criteria. Against each of the criteria, the Quality Assurance Function, having reviewed the products and evidence, records an overall quality assessment using a red/amber/green (RAG) method.

Once the Exit Criteria Checklist has been completed, the key learning points should be identified and made available to other programmes and projects in the form of lessons learnt.

5.10.2 Programme Board approval
With the preparation for implementation complete the Programme Board should decide whether implementation on the planned date should go ahead. The Programme Board should base its decision upon the status of the Go-live Assessment Report and the Phase 5 Exit Criteria Checklist.

If the Programme Board feels that the business and/or solution are not ready to be implemented, then the implementation date will be postponed and a new date set when the issue is expected to be resolved.

5.11 GO LIVE AND ENABLE BENEFITS
Purpose
This is it!
The solution now goes live and once everything has been successfully implemented, the Benefits are set to the status Enabled. We should now see that:
- Data is migrated
- New technology is enabled and the old systems are switched off
- Relocations take place and people take up their new roles
- People start using new processes guided by new policies, standards and procedures.

Stage 5.11 consists of the following activities:

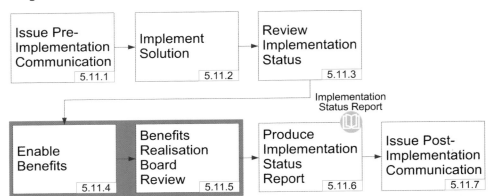

Figure II.5.14 – Activities in stage 5.11 – Go-live and Enable Benefits

5.11.1 Issue pre-implementation communication

Pre-implementation communication for staff, customers and interested parties, is designed to confirm that the implementation is going ahead and to clarify the sequence of events and any impact on normal operation. For example, there might be:

■ Disruption of service for a period of time
■ A freeze on data
■ An office move
■ Deadlines to close certain business activities before implementation.

The post-implementation support arrangements need to be clarified as well and relevant guidelines and contact details distributed.

5.11.2 Implement solution

The solution is fully implemented and the business switches to the new ways of working based on detailed implementation plans. Some parts of the solution would have been gradually implemented during transition. For example, infrastructure may have been set up, the workplace refurbished or people appointed to new jobs.

Throughout the implementation (which could be timed over a weekend or a quiet period for the business) there should be regular checks on status, progress against plans and immediate verification of completed tasks, for example, checking data migration counts and monitoring any problems encountered.

5.11.3 Review implementation status

The success of implementation cannot be judged purely by completion of implementation tasks against the plan. Look out for indications that:

■ Data has been migrated accurately
■ The main transactions that are required by the business are working
■ Interfaces are operating correctly
■ The infrastructure, such as network connections, printers or telephones, is working.

These tests are best accomplished within individual business areas, and will at the same time indicate which areas are fully operational and which are not. In the event that the solution does not fully work in all business areas and the problems cannot be immediately resolved, a decision has to be made whether to still declare the solution 'live' or revert to the old operation using a back out plan.

5.11.4 Enable Benefits

Assuming implementation has gone well, Benefits may now be promoted to Enabled status. Benefit Cards should be updated accordingly and signed by respective Benefit Owners. A new percentage confidence in the likelihood of realising the Benefit may be assigned at the same time.

Now it is up to business areas to make full use of new processes, technology and organisational changes and actually realise Benefits.

5.11.5 Benefits Realisation Board review

The Benefits Realisation Board has been following Benefits from their identification within phase 2 – Shaping and Planning through validation within phases 3 – Design and 4 – Service Creation and Realisation. Now the Board needs to be informed about:
- Which Benefits have been fully Enabled
- Whether all early Benefits have been Enabled, in other words Benefits that are expected to be measured shortly after implementation
- Whether there were any implementation issues affecting future Benefits realisation – for example, some aspects of the solution may not be fully operational.

5.11.6 Produce Implementation Status Report

The outcomes of implementation should be documented within the Implementation Status Report.

The report is distributed to key stakeholders who need to understand the impact of any outstanding issues – for example, the impact on customers or Benefits realisation.

Product title	Implementation Status Report	Phase 5
Purpose	To assess the success of implementation	
Description	The status immediately after implementation needs to be reviewed to assess the success of implementation activities, the availability of all the components of the solution and any outstanding issues	
Composition	■ Activities completed against implementation plan ■ Status of components ■ Status of business areas ■ Outstanding issues and actions	
Input from	Implementation plan	

Used as an input to	Decommissioning or back-out decisions
Approved by	Programme Board

Table II.5.3 – Implementation Status Report composition

5.11.7 Issue post-implementation communications

Communicating the success of the solution as soon as possible to the whole business and the Programme Teams is recommended. There are a number of key messages that should go out, including:

- Confirmation that the business solution went live successfully
- Confirmation of which business areas have gone live
- Prompts for personnel within the business areas, reminding them that they need to use the new solution
- Encouragement to use the new ways of working
- Re-iteration of the business Benefits of the new solution.

It is also worth thinking about opportunities to communicate that the new processes are now in place to stakeholders, customers and suppliers.

business. There may well be Benefits that emerge shortly after implementation. Others could take effect in weeks, months or a number of years. In this stage the Benefits Realisation Plan is updated to ensure that there is a record of how the business has benefited and where there are Benefits still to come.

Benefits realisation

A final stage in the Benefits management lifecycle when the Benefits are actually achieved.

Stage 6.2 consists of the following activities:

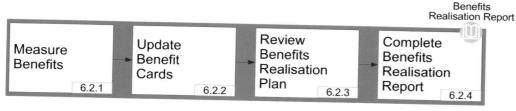

Figure II.6.3 – Activities in stage 6.2 – Realise Benefits

6.2.1 Measure Benefits

The majority of Benefits are likely to be achieved in phase 7 – Benefits Realisation. However, there may be some Benefits that can be measured soon after implementation. For example:

- Savings on software licences
- Terminating property leases
- Compliance with legislation
- Terminating old contracts.

Each Benefit should have a method of measuring the difference it will make and a target value defined on the Benefit Card. For example, it may be possible to measure customer satisfaction or the number of complaints received. Baseline data would have been collected before implementation. Now the data after implementation needs to be collected and a calculation made of the difference. The Benefit is then compared against the target value on the Benefit Card.

If an expected Benefit has not been fully achieved, the status on the Benefit Card remains Enabled and the reasons for this should be explored.

6.2.2 Update Benefit Cards

Once the Benefit has been measured and fully achieved, its status should be changed from Enabled to Realised and it should be signed by the Benefit Owner.

Often Benefits will be partially achieved, in which case a percentage of realisation should be recorded. If the Benefit has not been achieved, it should be left in the status Enabled with reasons, risks and agreed actions added to the Benefit Card.

6.2.3 Review Benefits Realisation Plan

The Benefits Realisation Plan needs to be revised regularly. There may also be occasions when a separate Benefits realisation project needs to be started. All changes to the Benefits Realisation Plan and predicted dates should be confirmed with Benefit Owners, and the Benefit Cards updated.

It is essential that people are made available within business areas who will perform the activities that support Benefits realisation. Where necessary this may mean:
■ Calculating and collecting relevant data on current performance against baseline
■ Analysing reasons if the Benefits have not been fully achieved
■ Identifying actions to ensure full Benefits realisation
■ Creating new, and amending existing, Realisation Plans

6.2.4 Complete Benefits Realisation Report

A Benefits Realisation Report should be produced summarising the status of Benefits to date and should include all the Benefits measured within the period. The Report should be sent to the Benefits Realisation Board and the Executive who approved the Full Business Case.

Product title	Benefits Realisation Report	Phase 6/7
Purpose	To assess achievements of anticipated Benefits	
Description	Benefits will be measured in predefined periods of time, as defined within the Benefits Realisation Plan. The findings will be documented within the Benefits Realisation Report, with suggested actions to address any under-achievement of Benefits	
Composition	■ Benefits measured this period and their expected and actual value ■ Reasons for under or over-achievement of Benefits ■ Actions to address under-achievement ■ Next Benefits realisation activities	
Input from	Benefit Card, Benefits Realisation Plan	
Used as an input to	Call Benefits Star Chamber	
Sent to	Benefits Realisation Board, Executive (information only)	

Table II.6.1 – Benefits Realisation Report composition

6.3 EXECUTIVE GATE

Purpose

Have we achieved what we expected?

In the short space of time since the solution went live the business may have achieved some Benefits. The Benefits Realisation Report will be reviewed by the:

- Programme Board
- Benefits Realisation Board
- Executives.

Stage 6.3 consists of the following activities:

Figure II.6.4 – Activities in stage 6.3 – Executive gate

6.3.1 Programme Board review

The Programme Board needs an early indication about the success of the solution. It will review the Benefits Realisation Report and compare the findings with Benefit Cards and the Full Business Case and approve any actions required to remedy under-achievement of Benefits or reduce the risks of future under-achievement.

6.3.2 Benefits Realisation Board review

The Benefits Realisation Board will receive feedback on the overall Benefits. They will be interested in an overview of how it is going, including:

- Matching the results against expected Benefits documented on Benefit Cards
- The contribution of these Benefits to the overall Benefits targets of the organisation
- The impact of any under-achievement of Benefits
- Projected Benefits realisation in the future and the impact on other Benefits.

6.3.3 Executive Review

The Executive review will be looking for reassurance that:

- The investment they approved in the Full Business Case is bringing the expected Benefits
- The business has made a significant step forward
- There is confidence in further Benefits realisation.

6.4 PROVIDE STABILISATION SUPPORT

Purpose

How well is the solution working?

Consideration now needs to be given to whether any further support is required to ensure that the solution is stabilised and improvements are identified.

Based on this information, appropriate improvements can be made to processes, organisation structure or technology.

Stabilisation support activities run in parallel with Benefits realisation.

This stage consists of the following activities:

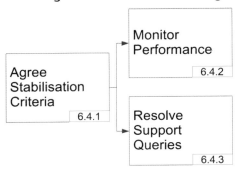

Figure II.6.5 – Activities in stage 6.4 – Provide stabilisation support

6.4.1 Agree stabilisation criteria

How well is the solution working? The answer should be worked up into a set of acceptance criteria for the end of the stabilisation period which should include:

- Business processes – are these in place and in use without a high level of assistance?
- Business documentation – are documents complete and stored appropriately?
- Business performance metrics – can the business areas reach defined and acceptable levels of performance?
- Organisation – are people working in their roles, teams and locations in the new organisation as expected?
- Training – has additional training been completed?
- Technology – are systems working without problems?
- Business support – are support people and systems able to provide support to the business team without the help of the Programme Team?

6.4.2 Monitor performance

Performance monitoring should be carried out at regular intervals. How well the solution is performing can be measured by, for example, analysing the types of queries raised by people who are using it and how these queries are resolved. Process monitoring could include gathering information on the daily/ weekly performance of the new processes, statistics on the number of users, how long queries take to resolve and so on. Technology monitoring might look at the availability of new systems during core hours, levels of activity on the new systems with response times and any scheduled outages. Appropriate changes should be initiated by specialist technology teams or the Programme Team.

Monitoring, maintaining and improving performance is the responsibility of business managers. The Programme Team should be on hand only to ensure people are actually using the new processes, that resources are optimised and that any adverse effects are minimised.

6.4.3 Resolve support queries

People in the business need to know exactly where they can go for support during the early stages of implementation. Problems are likely to be associated with business processes or technology and may be handled by a stabilisation support team. It may be possible to resolve them quickly with front line support staff; or they will need to be passed to specialists. Experts in processes or technology should handle all specialised incidents, carry out any necessary investigations, ensure changes are made and record any progress.

There may be some change requests that have to be postponed to phase 7 and go through a formal change approval process.

6.5 PROCESS AND ORGANISATION STABILISATION
Purpose
How well are the processes and organisation performing?
It is time to focus on how well the new ways of working and the organisation are performing under the new solution and make the necessary changes. Stabilisation will be supported by on-job support within the business areas and additional training.

Stage 6.5 consists of the following activities:

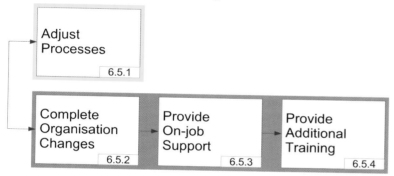

Figure II.6.6 – Activities in stage 6.5 – Process and organisation stabilisation

6.5.1 Adjust processes

Immediately after implementation the performance of business areas could actually go down. This, however, should improve as the stabilisation takes effect.

The majority of performance issues with new process can be attributed to lack of experience or training or there might be technical issues that hinder the process. Therefore, before any process is changed a question always needs to be asked as to whether the process has been fully and correctly used within the business area.

There might be a genuine reason to review some of the processes, for example, where bottlenecks occur or tasks can be further automated. In many cases it might be just documentation that needs changing, such as a procedure supporting the process might need to be documented to a greater level of detail to avoid misunderstandings.

6.5.2 Complete organisation changes

During stabilisation many of the organisational changes that have been delivered now need to be completed. The changes could involve:
■ Additional recruitment to find suitable people
■ Phasing out staff who were retained to keep operations running during implementation
■ Optimising roles and redefining duties or reporting lines
■ Changing locations of individuals or teams.

Any organisational changes may need to go through a period of consultation (activity 6.9.3).

6.5.3 Provide on-job support

People using the new solution in the business will inevitably have questions or concerns about the new ways of working. Some of these are best dealt with by local 'floorwalkers' or 'super users' who form part of the stabilisation effort managed by the Programme Team. They should provide a first and approachable contact point for new users to ask questions about the new processes or systems. They will also be able to:
■ Ensure people are using a consistent approach to the new processes and ways of working
■ Act as 'front-line' change agents and communicators with the business areas
■ Ensure that people have answers to their queries or issues
■ Ensure that people are using the support help desk.

All requests to the floorwalkers and the help desk should be logged and, where necessary, these requests should then be allocated to specialist groups for resolution.

6.5.4 Provide additional training

Ongoing training may still be needed where, for example, there are frequent mistakes or misunderstandings about processes and roles. Although most of the business areas would have been fully trained already, there could be a continuing need for training to cover staff who did not attend the original training sessions or to cover changes to the solution.

6.6 TECHNOLOGY STABILISATION
Purpose
How well is the technology solution performing?
It is at this point that the stabilisation of the technology solution is concluded, including fine-tuning the technology solution, decommissioning old systems and making minor fixes.

Stage 6.6 consists of the following activities:

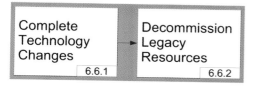

Figure II.6.7 – Activities in stage 6.6 – Technology stabilisation

6.6.1 Complete technology changes

In the initial period after implementation, users may experience a variety of 'teething' problems with the new technology, ranging from insufficient access rights to functionality or performance issues and system failures.

The issues will either be reported to the stabilisation support team or intercepted by the relevant technology area as part of operational support and monitoring.

These may result in:
- Quick fixes to resolve problems
- System or database tuning to optimise performance
- Improvements to provide a long-term resolution.

Some quick fixes such as access rights may be resolved directly by the business support team, whilst tuning and long term solutions will be delivered by specialist teams who will perform necessary investigations, make changes, test them and ensure that documentation is up to date.

At the end of phase 6 the technology should be sufficiently stable to meet the stabilisation criteria.

6.6.2 Decommission legacy resources

The introduction of a new solution, in many cases, means replacing existing technology or relocating technology to new buildings. Once the new operation is stable, and the old technologies are no longer needed, they can be decommissioned. For example, the new solution may require a different number of licences, and some licences may no longer be needed, or the old technology was needed for parallel running or a possible back out of the solution. Office space which is no longer needed or the services of an external supplier for example, may need to be decommissioned.

De-commissioning is important as it may contribute to tangible Benefits realisation such as efficiencies savings, reduced cost of software licences or lower costs for premises.

6.7 BUSINESS SUPPORT TRANSITION

Purpose

When does stabilisation support become business as usual support?

The temporary stabilisation support team was set up in stage 5.4. It is now time to hand over responsibility for supporting the delivered solution to the permanent support team. This may be an existing team in the business, which supports other business solutions.

Stage 6.7 consists of the following activities:

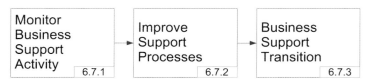

Figure II.6.8 – Activities in stage 6.7 – Business support transition

6.7.1 Monitor business support activity

At the end of stabilisation, support needs to be handed over to the business as usual support team. Before this can happen the support activity needs to be monitored. Depending on the stabilisation criteria this may, for example, include consideration of the:

■ Number of incidents – it is expected that this would fall as stabilisation progresses
■ Nature of incidents – it is expected that the severe incidents would have been resolved in the early days and the severity would be dropping
■ Performance of the support team – the support processes should operate smoothly for both business and technology aspects of support – for example, expected query resolution times.

These statistics feed into the improvement of support processes in stage 6.7.2 and stabilisation review at the end of phase 6.

6.7.2 Improve support processes

Based on the analysis of support activities there may be scope for improvement to ensure that the solution is appropriately supported in a number of areas:

■ Changes to support processes
■ Changes to the composition of the team
■ Changes to team size
■ Better tools for query resolution
■ Enhanced system access
■ Additional training
■ Better awareness of business needs
■ Better support documentation.

6.7.3 Business support transition

The handover of business support from the stabilisation support team to the business as usual support team requires a number of activities to happen:

■ Recruitment of additional members into business as usual support team
■ Training the business as usual team members in the relevant aspects of the solution
■ Training in the support processes and tools

- Consolidating documentation
- Setting up system accesses
- Knowledge transfer.

The most effective transition is likely to involve gradually replacing or overlapping the handover from members of the temporary support stabilisation team with members of the business as usual support team.

6.8 STABILISATION REVIEW
Purpose
Have we met our stabilisation criteria?
There will come a point when the stabilisation criteria need to be reviewed. This stage can be triggered either by a predefined time period stated within the stabilisation criteria or by meeting key indicators, such as the number of incidents dropping below a certain level. It is also important to check that the solution complies with legislation or any external or internal policies.

Stage 6.8 consists of the following activities:

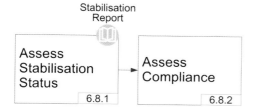

Figure II.6.9 – Activities in stage 6.8 – Stabilisation review

6.8.1 Assess stabilisation status
To review the how well the solution is working, a range of data should be analysed including:
- Performance reports from business areas
- Service level agreement reports
- Customer satisfaction surveys
- Incident reports from the support team
- Technical performance reports, such as availability and response times
- Financial reports.

The findings are documented with the Stabilisation Report that is submitted to the Programme Board.

Stabilisation Report
The Stabilisation Report is an assessment of whether the solution is stable enough to be supported by the business without assistance from the Programme Team.

Product title	Stabilisation Report		Phase 6
Purpose	To mark the end of the stabilisation period for the solution		
Description	An assessment of readiness to hand over the support of the solution from the Programme Team to the business as usual support team		

Composition	■ Stabilisation criteria
	■ Stabilisation status
	  □ Processes
	  □ Organisation
	  □ Technology
	■ Readiness to hand over business support		

Input from	Stabilisation criteria		
Used as an input to	Decision to hand over support to the business as usual support team		
Approved by	Programme Board		

Table II.6.2 – Stabilisation Report composition

6.8.2 Assess compliance

Compliance assessments have been performed throughout the whole lifecycle and this is the final check that all requirements have been met and all outstanding issues have been resolved or managed. The assessment includes:
■ Corporate strategies
■ External policies and legislation
■ Equality best practice.

A formal equality impact/needs assessment (EINA) may need to be carried out at this point to ensure that the newly implemented solution, including process, organisation and technology, meets the needs of different groups within the community and will not have any discriminatory outcomes. For example, it is important to ensure that new technologies are actually useable by customers or employees with a disability.

6.9 PROGRAMME BOARD GATE

Purpose

Is the solution now stable?

A primary objective of the Programme Board gate is to provide the Programme Board with a clear idea of how well the programme has performed in stabilisation and to carry out any final consultations before the programme comes to an end.

Stage 6.9 consists of the following activities:

Figure II.6.10 – Activities in stage 6.9 – Programme Board gate

6.9.1 Assess Phase 6 Exit Criteria

At the end of this phase the Quality Assurance Function performs an end-of-phase review on the programme using the Phase Exit Criteria Checklist. The Checklist describes the outcomes that are expected from the particular phase – irrespective of the actual approach or products. The criteria contained in all the Phase Exit Criteria Checklists are listed in appendix 2.

The Checklist asks for evidence of how the programme has met each of the criteria. Against each of the criteria, the Quality Assurance Function, having reviewed the products and evidence, will record an overall quality assessment using a red/amber/green (RAG) method.

Once the Exit Criteria Checklist has been completed, the key learning points should be identified and made available to other programmes and projects in the form of lessons learnt.

6.9.2 Programme Board approval

Based on the information in the Stabilisation Report, the Programme Board assesses the overall status of the solution and whether it is ready to hand over business support to the business as usual team. The Board is also looking to see whether the solution is working properly and that the expected early Benefits have been realised. If the solution is stable, the Programme Board should give approval for programme close-down.

6.9.3 Communication and consultation

Communication to stakeholders is important in all phases of CHAMPS2. Communication to staff at this point may centre on Benefits achieved and progress towards stabilising the solution. Customers also need to be informed of the changes they should see in services or products.

Key stakeholders, such as trade unions, productivity and performance groups, are likely to be interested in:
- Embedding the new solution within the business, including processes, organisation changes and technology
- Performance and stability of the new solution

- Achievement of performance indicators within business areas
- Realisation of initial Benefits and Benefits realisation trends
- Compliance with equality and diversity requirements.

Consultations may result in ideas for further improvements which can be put in place in phase 7 – Benefits Realisation.

6.10 PROGRAMME CLOSE-DOWN
Purpose
Are we ready to shut down the programme and hand over to the business?
Once stabilisation is complete the solution can be fully handed over to the business and the Programme closed down. But before the programme finishes it is worth looking back over the programme to consolidate lessons learnt.

Stage 6.10 consists of the following activities:

Figure II.6.11 – Activities in stage 6.10 – Programme close-down

6.10.1 Agree close-down checklist
Are we ready to close the programme? Completing the programme in a controlled and tidy manner can be achieved using a checklist covering:
- Handover – documentation on business support handover
- Benefits – confirming ownership of Benefit Cards and Benefits Realisation Plan
- Disbanding the team – PCs, system access, security badges, performing exit interviews
- Programme controls – closing accounts, timesheets, reporting mechanisms
- Workplace – emptying filing cabinets, handing over equipment, releasing office space.

6.10.2 Evaluate transformation journey
This is an internal review of the programme by the Programme Team to ascertain whether the programme has met its objectives and how effectively it has been managed.
This could be conducted as a workshop and the areas that should be considered are:
- Analysis of the whole programme against the Full Business Case
- Timescales and cost
- Programme and project management
- Design

- Solution creation and testing
- User acceptance testing and operational acceptance testing
- Transition
- Implementation
- Stabilisation
- Benefits management and early Benefits realisation.

The findings are documented and sent to the Programme Board for information.

6.10.3 Consolidate lessons learnt

Lessons learnt sessions are an ideal way to explore in a non-judgemental way:

- What worked well and should be adopted by other programmes
- What went less well and what should be avoided by future programmes
- How communication could be improved
- How future teams could operate more efficiently and effectively
- Other ideas that could help to accelerate or enhance other programmes can be captured
- How CHAMPS2 could be used more effectively.

The findings should be documented, made easily accessible and sent to relevant programmes and project functions within the organisation.

6.10.4 Business support handover

Business support is formally handed over from the stabilisation business support team to business as usual business support team. Many transitional activities will now be complete, such as:

- Recruitment of additional staff
- Training
- Getting documentation ready
- Setting up system accesses
- Knowledge transfer.

The final part of handing over knowledge needs to include:

- Business process documentation
- Technical documentation
- Support procedures.

Once business support is handed over, the temporary stabilisation support team can be disbanded.

6.10.5 Final handover to business

The final knowledge transfer from the Programme Team to the business should now take place and all the remaining documentation should be handed over.

The Design Blueprint, Functional and Technical Specifications will already have been handed over. In addition, other programme milestone documents need to be saved within the business, such as the Full Business Case or Product and Supplier Recommendations, to provide evidence for key decisions taken on the change journey.

Benefit ownership needs to be re-confirmed at this stage, making sure that there is a Benefit Owner for each Benefit Card, who will assume full responsibility for Benefits realisation. In addition a Business Realisation Plan Owner should be identified to facilitate the start-up of phase 7 and to continue to drive forwards with the overall Benefits Realisation Plan.

The owners of new business processes need to be clarified to ensure that any changes to the processes are agreed and sponsored by the business.

6.10.6 Disband Programme Team

Once the handover has been completed and the Programme Team's knowledge has been passed on to the business as usual business support team the Programme Team needs to be disbanded. There are a number of areas that need to be considered during this activity.

- Exit interviews
- Reassignment/redeployment
- Removing system access and access to buildings
- Clearing down personal repositories
- Stopping e-mail accounts
- Handing back equipment.

This now concludes the CHAMPS2 programme. However, the transformation change lifecycle will continue with phase 7 – Benefits Realisation.

PHASE 6 SUMMARY

In phase 6 the Programme Team hands the solution over to the newly formed Business support team. The business needs to agree that the solution is stable, take responsibility for delivering the remaining Benefits and look for ongoing improvements to enhance these.

Hints and tips

Stabilisation

Successful stabilisation and ongoing business support are critical foundations if the Benefits of the programme are to be achieved.

Benefits Realisation Plan

It is important to identify who will realise Benefits within business as usual once the programme team has been disbanded. The ownership of each Benefit should be confirmed. In other words, who will be responsible for the actual delivery of the Benefits within their business areas and also drive any Benefits realisation activities?

REFLECTIVE QUESTIONS

Reflective questions require you to examine your existing knowledge or experience before giving a thoughtful response.

There will be many activities in the initial period after implementation to stabilise the solution, embed new ways of working and realise Benefits. Support staff and expertise from the Programme Team need to be on hand.

1. Use your experience and your understanding of Go-live to analyse how performance can be affected immediately following implementation. What is the likely impact on: (a) employees, (b) customers, (c) stakeholders?.

2. What support should be in place to mitigate any issues during this period of stabilisation for employees?

3. Explain how communications can support people and customers during this period.

4. One of the potential issues during this period is that individuals find the changes hard to implement and start to revert to old ways of working. How does the CHAMPS2 method support the use of new ways of working?

Phase 7 – Benefits Realisation

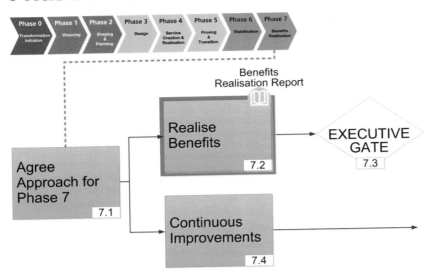

Figure II.7.1 – Phase 7 stages

Phase 7

This phase will ensure that any subsequent changes to the solution support the original Vision and that all Benefits are Realised.

PURPOSE OF PHASE 7 – BENEFITS REALISATION

The key objectives of phase 7 are:

- Achievement of Benefits that have been agreed at the beginning of the change programme
- Improvements to the solution, ensuring that these are in line with the overall Vision of the business area and that they support the Benefits realisation.

Once all the Benefits are realised, phase 7 comes to an end.

ROLES AND RESPONSIBILITIES

Business support team – A business as usual support team, which has taken over from the stabilisation support team in phase 6.

Benefits Realisation Board – Receives feedback on Benefits realisation.

Benefit Owner – Responsible for measuring Benefits realisation on the Benefit Card.

Benefits Realisation Plan Owner – Drives Benefits realisation across all Benefit Cards after the programme has been closed down.

Benefits Star Chamber – Resolves Benefits realisation issues by bringing together interested parties to remove barriers to Benefits realisation.

Executive – Reviews Benefits Realisation Report.

Quality Assurance Function – This group continues to provide advice and to monitor quality and the use of CHAMPS2.

7.1 AGREE APPROACH FOR PHASE 7
Purpose
How do we realise Benefits and continually improve?
It is important to review the path at the beginning of each phase to ensure that the activities are relevant and support the achievement of Benefits. This stage also includes a review of the continuous improvement process.

Stage 7.1 consists of the following activities:

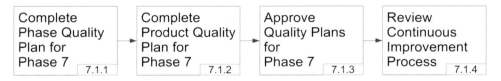

Complete Phase Quality Plan for Phase 7	Complete Product Quality Plan for Phase 7	Approve Quality Plans for Phase 7	Review Continuous Improvement Process
7.1.1	7.1.2	7.1.3	7.1.4

Figure II.7.2 – Activities in stage 7.1 – Agree approach for phase 7

7.1.1 – 7.1.3 Quality Plans
The approach for phase 7 is captured in two documents that are central to maintaining quality standards and managing client expectations:
- Phase Quality Plan – to tailor the stages and activities to the programme's needs
- Product Quality Plan – to ensure the quality of each product and how it is approved.

At the end of the phase the Phase 7 Exit Criteria Checklist is used to assess whether the phase objectives have been met. This document, therefore, forms a vital input into the development of Quality Plans and should be considered when the plans are being created. Lessons learnt from other change initiatives should be considered when choosing the most appropriate approach.

These are key products from the Quality Management Framework, which is fully explained in section III.

7.1.4 Review continuous improvement process
In order to ensure that Benefits are not lost any changes to the solution need to support Benefits realisation. The continuous improvement process should be reviewed at this point to specifically link back to the transformation programme. The process needs to:
- Assess all improvements against the programme's Vision, desired Outcomes and Benefits
- Look for additional Benefits to enhance Benefits realisation
- Incorporate any actions from Benefits realisation into continuous improvement
- Keep documentation delivered by the programme up to date
- Involve the Benefit Owners.

Once the process is agreed, Benefits realisation and continuous improvement can run in parallel.

7.2 REALISE BENEFITS

Purpose

What Benefits have we achieved so far?

Some Benefits will be realised shortly after implementation, others could take a number of years and will require ongoing monitoring. If the Benefit has not been fully achieved, appropriate action will have to be taken and the Benefits Realisation Plan updated accordingly.

This stage may be performed several times to correspond with the Benefits Realisation Plan. At the end of each Benefits realisation stage the results need to be fed back to the Benefits Realisation Board and Executive.

Stage 7.2 consists of the following activities:

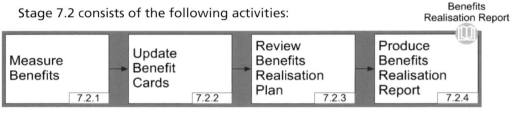

Figure II.7.3 – Activities in stage 7.2 – Realise Benefits

7.2.1 Measure Benefits

Measuring and evaluating the achievement of Benefits was initiated in stage 6.2.1 and should be an on-going process. Benefits achieved are compared with the expected Benefits documented on the Benefit Cards.

7.2.2 Update Benefit Cards

Once the Benefit has been measured and fully achieved, its status changes to Realised. Often Benefits are partially achieved, in which case a percentage of realisation should be recorded. The achievement of a Benefit should be signed by the Benefit Owner on the Benefit Card.

If the Benefit has not been achieved, it is left in the status Enabled. Reasons for not realising the Benefits and actions should be documented on the Benefit Card. Reasons could, for example, include external factors, dependencies on other programmes or the need to change some elements of the solution. In addition, if there were any risks identified that could jeopardise future Benefits, these should be highlighted on the Benefit Card.

Following any updates to Benefit Cards, Benefits Realisation Plans may need to be adjusted.

7.2.3 Review Benefits Realisation Plan

At the end of each Benefits realisation stage, the Benefits Realisation Plan needs to be revised:
■ In the light of the results of the latest Benefits evaluation and the resulting actions, there may be, for example, a need to introduce an additional Benefits realisation stage. This could include collecting a larger sample of data, or closer monitoring of some of the Benefits.

- Based on detailed planning for the next Benefits realisation stage, this may mean the initiation of a separate Benefits realisation project. The scope of the next Benefits realisation project will have to be confirmed, a schedule of events for data collection compiled, Benefits evaluation planned and the dates agreed.

It is also worth looking for further challenges to Benefits realisation and identifying any risks that could jeopardise Benefits realisation in the future.

All changes to Benefits Realisation Plans and the latest dates should be confirmed with the Benefits Realisation Plan Owner, who will be responsible for scheduling the next batch of Benefits realisation activities according to the plan.

7.2.4 Produce Benefits Realisation Report

At the end of each Benefits realisation period a report is also produced summarising the status of Benefits to date. The report should contain:
- Achievement of Benefits against the values agreed on Benefit Cards
- Reasons for under or over-achievement of Benefits
- Any issues identified and remedial actions
- Benefits Realisation Plan showing the next Benefits realisation period.

The Benefits Realisation Report is reviewed by the Programme Board and Benefits Realisation Board and it is also sent to the Executive who initially approved the Full Business Case.

7.3 EXECUTIVE GATE
Purpose
Have we achieved what we set out to do?
The Benefits Realisation Report is created by the Benefit Owner and the Benefits Realisation Plan Owner and reviewed by the Benefits Realisation Board and the Executive.

In case there are major discrepancies in Benefits Realisation, a Benefits Star Chamber may be called to resolve the situation.

Stage 7.3 consists of the following activities:

Figure II.7.4 – Activities in stage 7.3 – Executive gate

7.3.1 Benefits Realisation Board review

The Benefits Realisation Board will receive feedback on the overall Benefits. They will be interested in an overview of how it is going, including:

- Matching the results against expected Benefits documented on Benefit Cards
- The contribution of these Benefits to the overall Benefits targets of the organisation
- The impact of any under-achievement of Benefits
- Projected Benefits realisation in the future and the impact on other Benefits.

Any major issues with Benefits realisation should be escalated to the Benefits Star Chamber.

7.3.2 Benefits Star Chamber

If, for example, there are delays or Benefit values which do not match expected values, key stakeholders will be called to a Benefits Star Chamber meeting. These stakeholders could include heads of relevant functions, Benefits Owners, technology experts, suppliers and so on.

The reasons for under-achievement of Benefits should be discussed in the open, such as:

- Process flow issues
- Technology failures
- Non-compliance with the service level agreements between different parties
- Resourcing and skills issues
- Slow take-up of products and services by customers
- Poor quality of products or services.

The purpose of the Star Chamber meeting is to agree any actions to boost Benefits realisation and ensure that these are given high priority within relevant areas.

7.3.3 Executive Review

The results of each Benefits realisation stage should be submitted to the Executive, so that they can monitor and be confident of the achievement of the Outcomes identified in the Full Business Case. The Executive also needs to be aware of any remedial actions and, in particular, of those that require additional investment.

7.3.4 Assess Phase 7 Exit Criteria

This activity is performed only once, when phase 7 comes to an end. The Quality Assurance Function performs an end-of-phase review using the Phase Exit Criteria Checklist. The Checklist describes the outcomes that are expected from the phase – irrespective of the actual approach or products. The criteria contained in all the Phase Exit Criteria Checklists are listed in appendix 2.

Once the Exit Criteria Checklist has been completed, the key learning points should be identified and made available to other programmes and projects in the form of lessons learnt.

7.4 CONTINUOUS IMPROVEMENT

Purpose

What can we do better?

The purpose of this stage is to ensure that Benefits are sustainable, that the solution is improved and that the business does not return to the old ways of working.

Stage 7.4 consists of the following activities:

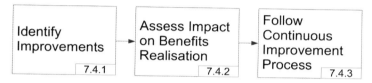

Figure II.7.5 – Activities in stage 7.4 – Continuous improvement

7.4.1 Identify improvements

Continuous improvement is likely to be an iterative process of identifying, assessing and delivering improvements. Potential improvements may be required because of:

- Issues reported to business support
- Performance issues
- Business managers identifying improvement ideas
- Customer feedback
- Requirements from other business areas
- New software/applications releases
- Learning from other organisations
- Legislation.

It is important that during Benefits realisation improvements contribute directly to the Benefits, Vision and strategic Outcomes agreed at the outset.

7.4.2 Assess impact on Benefits realisation

While Benefits realisation is in progress, all improvement ideas, irrespective of their origin, have to be assessed for their impact on overall Benefits realisation. It is not uncommon to find that once the solution has been implemented there will be a tendency to slowly revert to the old ways of working.

Therefore, where possible, any improvements should:

- Support the agreed Vision and strategic Outcomes
- Contribute towards Benefits Realisation
- Identify additional Benefits.

If there is an adverse impact on Benefits it should be agreed with Benefit Owners, and the Benefits Realisation Board should be notified.

7.4.3 Follow continuous improvement process

Actual improvements should be delivered using a standard continuous improvement process within the business. This typically involves:

- Selection of an appropriate delivery route, depending on the nature of change, for example: quick fix, small change or major improvement
- Assessment and prioritisation, which may take into account Benefits, risks, timescales, cost and any mandatory requirements
- Development of Business Cases if necessary
- Obtaining appropriate approval
- Delivering the change through business support arrangements or setting up a separate project.

Major improvements are likely to involve elements of process change, organisation change and technology change, or may even involve changes to the Future Operating Model. The nature of the additional changes should determine the stages and activities from CHAMPS2 that need to be revisited and planned for, and the products that need to be amended or developed.

PHASE 7 SUMMARY

In phase 7 the business takes responsibility for delivering the remaining Benefits. Plans for Benefits realisation need to be monitored regularly by the Benefits Realisation Plan Owner and the Benefit Owners. Ongoing improvements which will enhance the solution in practice should also be identified. It is important to ensure that these changes are carefully selected and prioritised, then delivered in the most efficient manner.

Hints and tips

Benefits realisation

Benefits realisation may well continue for some time. The process is now owned by the business and a sharp focus on the Vision and Benefits needs to be retained. Benefits should not be double counted and programmes should be sure what element of a Benefit they are expected to deliver and how the Benefit is dependent on other programmes or projects.

Improvements

It is vital that any further changes are in line with the Vision for the business area and support Benefits realisation. Include Benefits realisation as a standard feature of your improvement assessment process. Any changes or improvements required also need to be assessed for their impact on Benefits

Reflective questions

Reflective questions require you to examine your existing knowledge or experience before giving a thoughtful response

1. Keeping your focus on Benefits realisation is vital. What communications do you think you could provide to your own team and other areas of the business/stakeholders to inform them of your progress, celebrate success and mitigate risks?

2. How often should communications be sent out?

3. In what ways could you help to ensure that people do not return to old ways of doing things, especially in the short term after implementation?

Section III
CHAMPS2 Themes

SECTION III – CHAMPS2 THEMES

Objectives of this section

After reading this section you will understand:

1. The purpose of the CHAMPS2 **Quality Management Framework** and the products, activities, roles and responsibilities involved.

2. CHAMPS2 **governance** including gates and products, strategies and the roles and responsibilities.

3. **Benefits management** and monitoring, why this is important in CHAMPS2 and how the roles and responsibilities and strategies support this.

Chapter 1 – Quality Management Framework

Quality Management Framework

The CHAMPS2 Quality Management Framework provides a structured approach, as well as consistency and standards for transformational change. It is also used to help tailor CHAMPS2 to an individual programme.

This chapter explains:
- *The purpose of the Quality Management Framework*
- *The key products and activities*
- *Sharing best practice*
- *Roles and responsibilities.*

PURPOSE OF THE QUALITY MANAGEMENT FRAMEWORK

The Quality Management Framework brings a consistency of approach and supports the use of the CHAMPS2 method in the most effective and efficient way. It helps organisations to:
- Choose the right path
- Ensure the quality of products
- Check the achievements at the end of the phase
- Manage quality through a common strategy
- Incorporate quality assurance
- Incorporate lessons learnt
- Evaluate the transformation journey.

This is achieved through the products and activities in the following diagram:

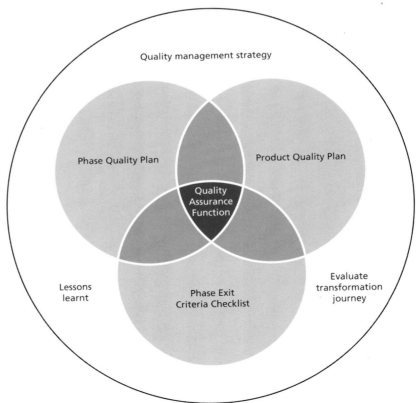

Figure III.1.1 – Key quality management products and activities

THE KEY PRODUCTS AND ACTIVITIES

At the core of the framework are three products:

- **Phase Quality Plan** – describes the CHAMPS2 process tailored to the individual programme's needs
- **Product Quality Plan** – describes the products to be delivered during a particular phase and their review and approval path
- **Phase Exit Criteria Checklist** – a review checklist which ensures that the outcomes of the phase have been met and that the programme is ready to move to the next phase.

Templates for these products can be downloaded from the CHAMPS2 Knowledge Centre at www.champs2.info

Phase Quality Plan

The Phase Quality Plan defines which activities will be performed and to what standards, and identifies which products are to be delivered during the phase. It must be developed and approved for each phase in advance of any delivery work starting.

Product title	Phase Quality Plan
Purpose	To assure quality and tailor CHAMPS2 to programme needs
Description	The Phase Quality Plan allows Programme Teams to define which activities will be performed during the phase, what approach will be taken for each and which products will be delivered as part of that approach. The approach taken must satisfy the Phase Exit Criteria Checklist used at the end of the phase
Composition	A list of stages and activities within the phase containing: ■ Suggested approach ■ Suggested products ■ Indicator whether activity is to be selected or removed ■ Alternative approach ■ Alternative products
Input from	Phase Quality Plan template, Phase Exit Criteria Checklist
Used as an input to	Product Quality Plan, programme and project plans
Approved by	Senior Responsible Owner, Quality Assurance Function, Programme Manager (phases 3 to 6)

Table III.1.1 – Phase Quality Plan composition

The Phase Quality Plan is the CHAMPS2 tool used to select the path through CHAMPS2 that suits the individual change programme. It records where activities have been taken out or added in. This should be a conscious decision-making process, and it should be recognised that there are risks in taking activities out. The same approach should be adopted even for small programmes or component projects under the control of a Programme Board.

The standard activities from CHAMPS2 and their possible products are listed in the Phase Quality Plan. It is developed by showing which of these standard activities will be performed and which will not. The Phase Quality Plan also lists the standard products that could be produced, alongside each standard activity.

Where there are multiple streams of work involved, typically from phase 3 – Design onwards, the Phase Quality Plan should also indicate which activities are performed at programme level, producing a single product, and which activities are performed at work stream level, producing a separate product for each work stream or project. This master Phase Quality Plan will then form the basis for creating individual quality plans later in the phase as the individual work streams or projects are planned in detail.

Additional activities that are not part of the standard method may be inserted into the plan. For example, a proof of concept may be needed within phase 3 – Design that will require some of the activities from phase 4 – Service Creation and Realisation.

Process for completing the Phase Quality Plan
1. Download the template for the relevant Phase Quality Plan.
2. Review each item on the list one by one and consider whether it is required or not.
3. Add any further activities specific to the programme.
4. Fill in the reasons for any changes to the plan.
5. Identify an alternative product if a standard product is not going to be used.
6. List the work streams and indicate in which work stream the activities will be performed and the products produced. Alternatively indicate whether the product is programme-wide.

The Phase Quality Plan (or a master Phase Quality Plan) should be approved by the Senior Responsible Owner, Programme Manager (phases 3 to 6) and the Quality Assurance Function. Where there are multiple work streams involved it is only the master Phase Quality Plan that requires this level of approval.

Phase Quality Plan										
Stage/ Activity No.	Stage/ Activity Description	Approach	Possible Product/s	Use Stage/ Activity (Y/N)	Approach (If non-standard)	Possible Product/s (If non-standard)	Programme Level	Work Stream 1	Work Stream 2	Work Stream 3

Figure III.1.2 – Part of the Phase Quality Plan template

Product Quality Plan

The Product Quality Plan defines and describes each product to be produced by the programme during each particular phase. It must be developed and approved for each phase in advance of delivery work starting.

Product title	Product Quality Plan
Purpose	To assure the quality of products
Description	The Product Quality Plan defines the acceptance criteria and review /approval path for products identified within Phase Quality Plan
Composition	A list of products delivered within the phase containing: ■ Product description ■ Acceptance criteria ■ Persons accountable and responsible for product delivery ■ Reviewers of the product ■ Person accountable for approval and acceptance of the product
Input from	Phase Quality Plan, Product Quality Plan template
Used as an input to	Product breakdown structure, project plans
Approved by	Senior Responsible Owner, Quality Assurance Function, Programme Manager (phases 3 to 6)

Table III.1.2 – Product Quality Plan composition

All products to be produced should be named on the Product Quality Plan. There may be many products developed during a phase and it may not be appropriate to keep presenting each individual product for review or approval. In such cases, the products may be combined into a new product or deliverable. The product plan would still need to show each individual product and the named deliverable.

Where there are multiple streams of work involved, typically from phase 3 – Design onwards, a master Product Quality Plan is produced at the beginning of the phase, corresponding to a master Phase Quality Plan. This will form the basis for creating individual Product Quality Plans later in the phase as the individual work streams or projects are planned in detail.

Process for using the Product Quality Plan

1. Download the template for the relevant Product Quality Plan.
2. Follow the headings and amend the activities and products to match the Phase Quality Plan.
3. Enter the product description and the acceptance criteria for the product.
4. Enter who is accountable and responsible.

5. Enter who will review and approve the product.
6. For a master Product Quality Plan approvals may be expressed as levels – i.e. Level 1 Executive; Level 2 Programme Board; Level 3 Programme Manager etc. Approval levels are defined within the quality management strategy within phase 2 – Shaping and Planning.
7. For detailed Product Quality Plans exact names should be entered
8. Identify in which work stream the product will be produced.

Product Quality Plan												
Stage/ Activity No.	Stage/ Activity Description	Product	Product Description	Acceptance Criteria	Account-able	Responsible	Reviewers	Approver	Programme Level	Work Stream 1	Work Stream 2	Work Stream 3

Figure III.1.3 – Part of the Product Quality Plan template

Phase Exit Criteria Checklist

At the end of each delivery phase, and prior to starting the next phase, the Quality Assurance Function will perform an end of phase review on each programme using the relevant Phase Exit Criteria Checklist. The criteria contained in all the Phase Exit Criteria Checklists are listed in appendix 2.

Product title	Phase Exit Criteria Checklist
Purpose	To check whether the outcomes of the phase have been achieved
Description	A checklist to ensure that the outcomes of the phase have been achieved, supported by evidence of products and key decisions. The checklist is also used to check the readiness to move to the next phase
Composition	■ Phase Exit Criteria ■ Evidence that criteria have been met ■ Comments /observations ■ Quality status
Input from	Phase Quality Plan, Product Quality Plan
Used as an input to	Programme status reported to Programme Board, next phase
Approved by	Senior Responsible Owner, Quality Assurance Function

Table III.1.3 – Phase Exit Criteria Checklist composition

The purpose of this product is two-fold. The Checklist assesses whether the programme has delivered what it said it would and that everything needed to start the next phase is in place. Evidence, in the form of interviews, for example, may be required to check that people understand the products that have been created or the impact of changes.

Process for completing the Phase Exit Criteria Checklist
1. Download the relevant Phase Exit Criteria Checklist. Each phase in CHAMPS2 has an associated Checklist. It describes the Outcomes that are expected from the particular phase – irrespective of the actual approach or products.
2. Against each criteria, enter comments about how the criteria have been met and what evidence is available. It shows which products and outcomes address which particular criteria
3. A red/amber/green (RAG) assessment can be entered. Each criterion is assessed using a RAG scoring according to the scale below:

Green – criterion has been met
Amber – criterion has been partially met
Red – criterion has not been met

The Phase Exit Criteria Checklists are not intended to be policing documents. They are all available to all programmes at all times, so that there should not be any surprises at the end of any phase. They are designed to be a risk-prevention device so that programmes do not progress to the next phase leaving anything overlooked or without having obtained sufficient clarity. In nearly all cases, if criteria are skipped over, the issues they raise do not go away, but come back with negative consequences later.

Phase Exit Criteria Checklist			
Criteria	Evidence	Comments/Observations	Quality R/A/G

Figure III.1.4 – Part of the Phase Exit Criteria Checklist template

SHARING BEST PRACTICE
Quality management strategy
The quality management strategy could be programme-specific and created in stage 2.11, or there may be an existing quality management strategy within the organisation that could be used. It should define a common approach to applying quality across the programme, including:

- The structure of Product Quality Plans, which can be created at any level within the programme structure, such as project level, work stream level or programme level
- Review and approval levels – for example, level 1 might be peer review and level 5, Programme Board

- Roles and responsibilities
- Quality assurance process
- Escalation of quality issues
- Quality monitoring and reporting.

In addition, the strategy should include a method of monitoring the effectiveness of quality management within the programme.

Lessons learnt

At the end of each phase the Programme Team should review the lessons learnt from the programme. These should be shared across work streams and across programmes. At the beginning of each phase, lessons learnt from past experience should be considered.

Transformation journey evaluation

The transformation journey evaluation (stage 6.10) builds on the assessment of both the solution performance and how effectively the programme was managed. It covers:

- How well the programme was implemented in terms of time, cost, quality and early Benefits delivery
- Assessment against baseline information from the Full Business Case for each project or programme
- Whether the programme conformed to CHAMPS2 and the effectiveness of the programme management
- Whether the programme was effective in managing the change process and whether the different groups involved were able to co-operate
- What went well and why
- What could have been done differently
- What can we learn from the programme that could be used in the future?

ROLES AND RESPONSIBILITIES

Quality Assurance Function – A team of people dedicated to ensuring that the Programme Team adequately defines the products and activities required to deliver the solution and Benefits and check that quality criteria are set and met. The Quality Assurance Function may change in shape and size through the lifecycle, but will be required in every phase. The key products reviewed by the Quality Assurance Function are the:

- Phase Quality Plan
- Product Quality Plan
- Phase Exit Quality Checklist.

Senior Responsible Owner and Programme Manager – the Senior Responsible Owner and the Programme Manager are responsible for checking and approving all the Quality Plans to ensure that they contribute to strategic and programme objectives.

Chapter 2 – CHAMPS2 governance

CHAMPS2 governance

Governance consists of bodies (persons or committees) overseeing the transformation journey and key change management strategies.

This chapter explains:
- *CHAMPS2 gates and products*
- *CHAMPS2 strategies*
- *CHAMPS2 roles and responsibilities*
- *Design Authorities*
- *Benefits realisation governance.*

CHAMPS2 governance is about being in control of change and approving progress step by step. It is important that governance is visible and that products and activities are reviewed at major predefined points.

Everyone in the CHAMPS2 programme needs to know not only who to communicate with, but also when and what to communicate. This chapter explores structures for governance, communication and decision-making.

The formal governance approach has three principal functions:
- To champion the change programme providing visible and organised commitment to the need and Vision for change
- To ensure that the programme is managed effectively, efficiently and with minimum risk
- To provide a clear pathway for decision-making. For example, to release funding and check progress.

CHAMPS2 GATES AND PRODUCTS

CHAMPS2 uses a clear set of gates, to provide checks and balances and a number of core roles and responsibilities. In Figure III.2.1 you can see the key players. Their roles are described in brief below.

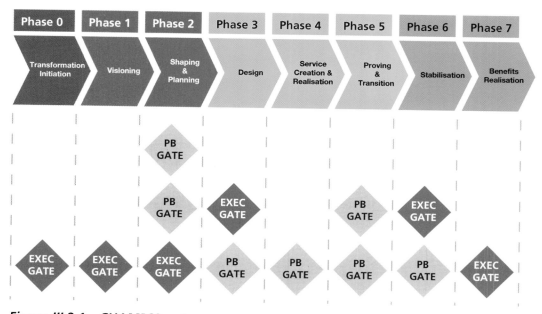

Figure III.2.1 – CHAMPS2 gates process

Executive and Programme Board gates

To increase the chances of success and to maintain a consistent Vision and Outcomes, there are two types of gate which provide direction to the whole process.

Executive gate

The Executive is called on periodically, but particularly in the early and late phases, to make the initial investment decision and to check return on investment in the form of Benefits.

Typically, the Executive is made up of senior leaders in the business with a clear view of the strategic needs of the organisation and its customers. They will be involved in championing the programme and communicating the Outcomes to be achieved.

The Executive takes key decisions in phases 0, 1 and 2, when they will assess the strategic Outcomes and strategic Benefits against the indicative cost and decide on funding options. Members also assess the effect of the proposed transformational change in the context of other transformational change programmes or other initiatives within the organisation. They will decide whether the Vision expresses what they want to achieve and whether the Future Operating Model encapsulates a new way forward for the business. The Executive reviews whether the risks, costs and timescales are manageable and approves the overall design for the new ways of working.

At the other end of the process the Executive is concerned with return on investment and whether the programme has met the Outcomes and Benefits.

Programme Board gate

The Programme Board oversees the programme delivery. The fundamental role of members is to review how well the programme is doing and to release funding at pre-defined points to allow transformational change to continue. There are gates at the end of every phase with defined milestone and transformational products that allow the Programme Board to understand and check progress.

CHAMPS2 STRATEGIES

The approach taken through CHAMPS2 will vary for any organisation depending on the size and nature of the transformational change. Whatever approach is used it is vital that the strategies for both how the programme is run and the nature of transformational change are considered, documented and used to set the direction for the programme.

Stage 2.11 asks us to determine the key strategies shown below. This may involve writing new strategies or making reference to existing strategies or good practice within the organisation. These will be refined and referred to throughout the programme. Remember that the strategic direction of the programme is also considered in phases 0 and 1 in terms of the way leaders want to approach and structure transformational change. The direction and approach for managing all elements of the way the programme is managed is also considered in the first stage of each phase, where Phase and Product Quality Plans are created.

The strategies that specifically provide direction for the way change is managed are the:

- **Training strategy**

  The training strategy needs to be developed to ensure that the new ways of working are supported by a comprehensive training programme for the business during the transition period and beyond.

- **Change management strategy**

  A change management strategy defines how the change is implemented into the business. This includes any phasing of projects or programmes to minimise the risk and reduce the impact of preparing people for change.

- **Benefits management strategy**

  The Benefits management strategy defines the approach to Benefits identification, tracking and realisation. It also defines roles and responsibilities in Benefits management.

- **Knowledge transfer strategy**

  To successfully implement the new ways of working within the business, the knowledge transfer strategy focuses on gradually handing over information and understanding to ensure that once the Programme Team is dissolved there is sufficient capability within the organisation to support the solution.

- **Communication strategy**

  The communication strategy is developed to cover communications within the programme, across other programmes, to the programme's Senior Responsible Owner, as well as to customers and to other stakeholders.

- **Testing strategy**

  The testing strategy document includes the overall approach for testing, the number of test phases, their frequency, concurrency, and other project limiting/constraining factors.

The strategies that provide direction for the way the programme is managed are:

- **Monitoring strategy**

  Monitoring the progress of the programme and projects should be planned carefully and associated reporting mechanisms are required.

- **Risk and issue management strategy**

  The risk and issue management strategy sets the framework for risk management for the whole programme. It defines the rules on how the organisation's standard risk and issue management method is applied to the programme.

- **Resource management strategy**
  The resource management strategy defines common accounting procedures to monitor cost and expenditure against expenditure approval processes and limits and financial reporting requirements. It also defines technologies and the format of information to be used in the process.

- **Quality management strategy**
  The quality management strategy defines a common approach to applying the Quality Management Framework across the programme and the quality management process.

CHAMPS2 ROLES AND RESPONSIBILITIES

Some people will stay with the programme throughout the course of the change; some, on the other hand, will come and go as progress is made through the different phases. It is important to know who the key decision-makers are at each point in the journey through the programme and provide them with the right information.

Illustrated below are two models for roles within the CHAMPS2 transformation lifecycle. The first is a basic model and the second a model which adds a further layer of control and management for larger scale transformational change.

Basic model

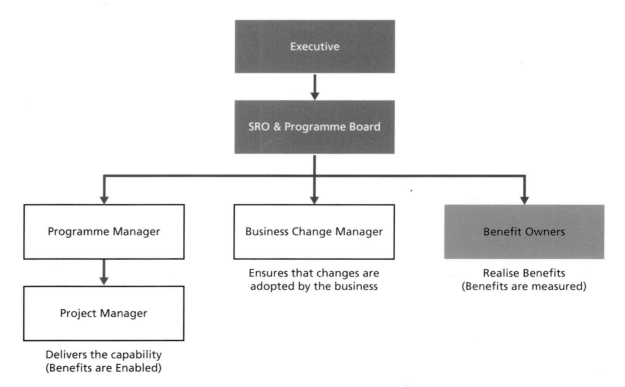

Figure III.2.2 – CHAMPS2 basic roles and responsibilities

Roles and responsibilities within the basic model of CHAMPS2 are as follows:

Executive
- Set strategic direction
- Approve programme direction
- Approve investment

Programme Board
- Provide leadership and direction to programme
- Ensure programme's alignment with organisation's strategic direction
- Release investment
- Approve progress through gates

Senior Responsible Owner (SRO)/Sponsor
- Provide leadership and direction to programme
- Ensure programme's alignment with organisation's strategic direction
- Accountable for Outcomes

Programme Manager
- Manage the programme to deliver desired Outcomes and Benefits
- Monitor programme's progress
- Manage risks, issues and interdependencies between projects

Project Manager
- Manage the project to deliver capabilities
- Monitoring project progress
- Manage project risks, issues and dependencies

Business Change Manager
- Identify, define and track the Benefits
- Prepare business operations for new ways of working
- Embed new business structures, operations and working practices

Benefit Owner
- Accountable for Benefits realisation of specific Benefits
- Responsible for Benefits drivers, for example, budget cuts, releasing staff and so on

Table III.2.1 – Roles and responsibilities within CHAMPS2 (basic)

Larger change initiatives

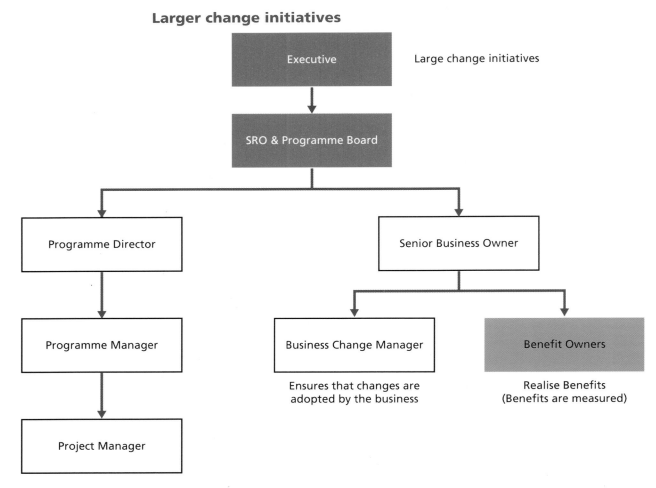

Figure III.2.3 – CHAMPS2 larger change initiatives roles and responsibilities

Additional roles and responsibilities within larger CHAMPS2 initiatives are as follows:

Programme Director ■ An optional role to take over some of the Senior Responsible Owner's responsibilities related to directing the programme
Senior Business Owner ■ An optional role to take over some of the Senior Responsible Owner's responsibilities to provide leadership within business areas affected

Table III.2.2 – Additional roles and responsibilities within larger CHAMPS2 initiatives

Beyond the roles and structures, the CHAMPS2 programmes will involve teams. The core teams are consistent, but the make-up of the teams may vary over the course of the transformation programme.

Chapter 3 – Benefits management

Benefits management

A structured approach to ensuring the delivery of business Benefits and tracking their journey from identification to Benefits realisation.

This chapter covers:
- *What Benefits are and why they are important*
- *Where do they fit in, in the transformation journey?*
- *Benefits lifecycle*
- *Benefits management*
- *Roles and responsibilities.*

WHAT ARE BENEFITS WITHIN CHAMPS2?

Benefits

Benefits are the difference transformation will make for the business and its customers.

It is important to be specific about Benefits or else it could become impossible to measure whether they have been achieved. This means being specific about the difference that needs to be made. Benefits can be categorised as financial, such as efficiency savings, or non-financial, such as an increase in customer satisfaction.

Financial Benefits or efficiency gains can be further viewed as cashable and non-cashable.
- Cashable efficiencies release financial resources whilst maintaining outputs and output quality, thereby enabling the resources that are released to be re-invested in other services or products. An example of this would be processing the same number of applications at a lower cost.

- Non-cashable efficiency gains are possible when volume or quality increases, either when the same resource is put in, or proportionately fewer resources, without releasing financial resources. An example of this would be processing an increased number of applications for the same cost.

Below are some more examples of Benefits:

The difference that the Benefit will make	Type of Benefit
Reduction of spending for the same product of service	Cashable
Reduction of prices for the same product or service	Cashable
Get more products or improved quality for the same price	Non-cashable
Get better service or improved quality in return for a proportionately smaller increase in resources	Non-cashable

Table III.4.1 – Examples of Benefits

Why do we need to define Benefits?
There are three principal reasons for defining Benefits within CHAMPS2.

1 Making a difference
Transformational change is ultimately led by the Vision and desired Outcomes. However, there is no point in undertaking a costly transformation programme if the business is already close to its Vision and desired Outcomes, or if the Vision or Outcomes are not challenging enough. It is the difference that matters.

Customers and staff will judge the success of transformation by the magnitude and value of change they see. They need to see a different business, a new business. Most organisations are seeking to do more with less and that means cashable and non-cashable Benefits.

2 Justifying transformation
Benefits are the key element of a Full Business Case. To justify the change programme a Full Business Case must be produced that puts the required investment into an equation with the Benefits that will be achieved by the investment. That will allow leaders to make a judgement on whether the investment is worth it.

3 Proving success
At the end of the transformation journey Benefits can be measured and they will be used to prove the success of the change programme. But it is not just at the end of the journey that success is measured; progress towards Benefits should be monitored.

The more accurately Benefits are defined, the more accurately they can be apportioned to different programmes or projects within a programme. Benefits are a key success measure for a programme and it is the responsibility of the Benefits Realisation Board to ensure that Benefits are not double counted by programmes and are apportioned correctly.

HOW BENEFITS FIT INTO THE TRANSFORMATION JOURNEY
Benefits drive the transformation journey and determine what outputs and changes are needed. The thinking has to start from the strategic Outcomes, as illustrated on the diagram below, and work backwards.

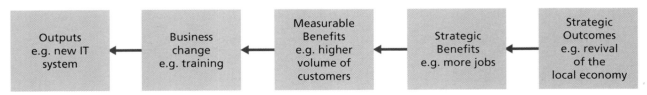

It is common for organisations to start with the solution (such as an IT system, a new facility or a new process) and then look for the Benefits to justify it – this is a fundamental flaw and often a reason for change initiatives failing.
A Benefits map can be used to document how Benefits relate to each other and the outputs required to deliver each Benefit. It is important to remember that the Benefits determine what outputs and changes are needed.

BENEFITS LIFECYCLE

Benefits realisation is at the heart of CHAMPS2. It is a Vision led, Benefits driven process. Benefits are embedded into the method, reviewed in every phase and encapsulated in four status stages.

Identified	Benefits defined, value calculated, assumptions documented, measurement process identified – % confidence value assigned
Validated	Benefits definition refined and value calculated as the level of understanding of the solution increases – for example, during phase 3 – Design, and phase 4 – Service Creation and Realisation – % confidence value reviewed
Enabled	The solution is ready and Benefits are reviewed to check whether it actually gets implemented and the business takes advantage of the Benefits – % confidence value evaluated again
Realised	Benefits are converted into savings or improved performance, i.e. staff are actually released and the budget reduced or the building is actually sold or the customer survey shows the desired difference in customer satisfaction – % realisation value achieved

Table III.4.2 – Benefit status stages

Within the CHAMPS2 Benefits management process each Benefit has a lifecycle of its own. It can be realised at its own pace, if it is not dependent on other later or earlier Benefits. Management of Benefits is facilitated by Benefit Cards, which include a summary of all the relevant information, assumptions and dependencies. One Benefit is recorded on each Benefit Card and each card is assigned an owner who is responsible for seeing the Benefit through to realisation.

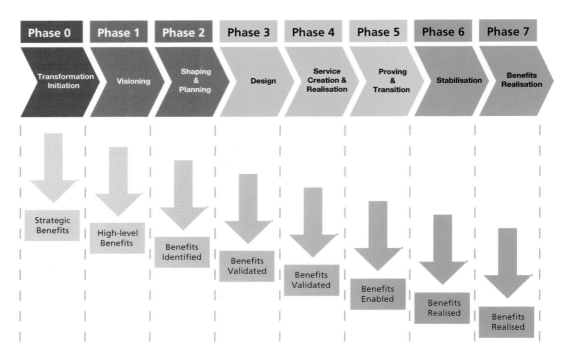

Figure III.4.1 – Phase view of Benefits realisation

Initial thoughts about Benefits originate from the beginning of the transformation journey when the business needs are identified and the Vision and Future Operating Model are formed. The focus at this point is on strategic Benefits, often defined in intangible terms, such as better service or higher staff morale.

In phase 2 the Benefits are made more concrete and measurable Benefits are defined.

Identifying Benefits
Benefits should be defined in a SMART way. They should be Specific, Measurable, Achievable, Realistic and Time-bound.

For example, how would you convert 'higher staff morale' into a more tangible statement of Benefits? The answer could be that measurements could be made about increased staff retention, lower absenteeism or a reduction in recruitment costs. These statements can be made SMART by stating which business areas they apply to and assigning realistic and achievable targets, such as 15% increase in staff retention by a specific date.

The identification of Benefits involves:
- Analysing current performance against benchmarks
- Agreeing Benefit types (financial/non-financial, cashable/non-cashable)
- Estimating the value of potential Benefits
- Developing a Benefits inventory
- Prioritising which Benefits are worth measuring.

A Benefit's value might be calculated as follows:

Driver	Target	Baseline	Improvement	Multiplier	Benefit
Average number of absent days per person per year	6.5 days	11.0 days	4.5 days	£150 per man day 2,367 days (full time equivalent)	£1,598K

Table III.4.3 – Calculating Benefits

Assumptions
1. Average full time equivalent cost is £33,000.
2. Average available work days per year = 220: one working day = £150.
3. There is always available work to be done.
4. Benefit is calculated using budgeted headcount for previous year of 2,367 days full time.
5. Baseline is full previous year.

The identified Benefit is recorded on a Benefit Card. The card includes the definition of the Benefit, measures, assumptions and dependencies on other Benefits. It should also include a percentage rating indicating confidence that the Benefit value will be achieved.

Each Benefit requires a Benefit Owner from the business, typically a budget holder, who is responsible for converting Benefits into reality. Benefit Owners need to understand where the Benefit has come from and be committed to taking appropriate action. For example, the financial savings may require the release of staff or office space. The Benefits to customers may be dependant on effective use of new processes or technology.

Validating Benefits
The Benefits identified within phase 2 – Shaping and Planning were based on a number of assumptions reflecting the level of understanding at the beginning of the transformation journey. During phase 3 – Design it may be discovered, for example, that some of the current processes can be omitted, giving rise to additional Benefits, or that the part of the solution has limitations that will reduce the anticipated Benefits.

In other words, as our level of understanding increases all Benefits are validated.

The questions to be asked include:
- Is the baseline data still valid?
- Are the assumptions still correct?
- Are any other business areas affected?
- What are the new timescales?
- Are there any new barriers to Benefits delivery?
- Are there any new dependencies?

Any changes to Benefits should be agreed with respective Benefit Owners and the Benefits Realisation Board. This may result in changes to the Full Business Case and the Benefits Realisation Plan.

Where there are cost implications the Benefits Realisation Board and the Executive may ask:
■ Are the Benefits still worth the investment?
■ Are the overall Outcomes still achievable?
■ Is the programme and level of change still affordable?

Benefits are re-validated in phase 4 once the solution has been built. Benefits remain at the Validated status until they are used in live operations. At this point, evidence is required that Benefits will eventually be realised and that barriers are removed.

Enabling Benefits
Benefits have been identified, Benefits have been validated – it is now time to deliver them.

This involves:
■ Implementing new processes
■ Installing the new technology and systems
■ Establishing the new organisation

Once all the components are in place Benefits realisation can start in earnest. It may be that there are several projects within the programme, which enable several Benefits at the same time. Benefit Cards are upgraded to Enabled and the percentage confidence levels are also hopefully upgraded.

Realising Benefits
Once the solution is in place, the Benefit Owner needs to ensure that Benefits materialise. For example, the new processes may require fewer resources or smaller office space. However, the financial savings will be made only if the staff are actually moved to the different business areas or the office space is actually released. Likewise, the Benefits to customers will become real only if the new processes are actually used.

At the end of the transformation journey, in phases 6 and 7, it needs to be proved that the Benefits have been achieved – this may not happen immediately; it can take months, or even years. Proving Benefits will typically involve comparing the data before and after transformation and calculating the 'actual' Benefits, which can then be evaluated against 'expected' Benefits. All activities associated with the collection of data and the evaluation of Benefits would have been planned in a Benefits Realisation Plan.

BENEFITS MANAGEMENT
Because Benefits are so important in CHAMPS2, it is essential that they are managed to ensure they are realised as originally intended. A Benefits management process must run throughout the change programme led by the Benefits Realisation Board and Benefit Owners.

Benefits management ensures that the Benefits have been clearly defined at the outset, that they are measurable, and that there is a commitment to their delivery from the business.

Benefits management strategy

Each programme requires a Benefits management strategy, created in stage 2.11, that should:

- Define the process for reviewing, updating and changing Benefit details, including who will be involved, how they will be involved and when reviews will be carried out
- Determine the project management approach, establishing whether the Benefits realisation occurs within the existing delivery project or whether a separate Benefits project is required. As a result of this, the project portfolio will be refined to include the necessary Benefits realisation projects
- Define the process for measurement, assessment and review of Benefits and Benefits realisation, including who will be involved, how they will be involved and when reviews will be carried out
- Define the roles and responsibilities required.

Benefits Realisation Plan

Benefits will also need to be considered during programme planning so that the programme structure reflects the dependency of Benefits realisation on delivery of individual projects, or groups of projects, within the project portfolio.

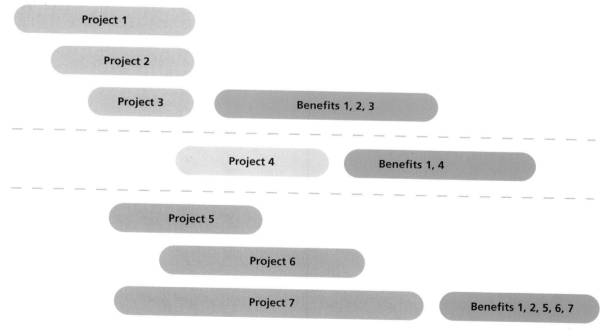

Figure III.4.2 – High-level programme structure

Some Benefits will be realised immediately after the solution goes live, whilst others will have longer Benefits realisation periods, beyond when the project or programme closes down. In either case, appropriate Benefits realisation projects need to be included in the project portfolio.

Activities related to realisation should be planned, such as:
- Collecting data for measuring Benefits

- Calculating the Benefits value
- Evaluating the achievement of Benefits
- Taking up actions to support full achievement of Benefits.

Monitoring Benefits

How do we ensure that they stay in line with the project plan throughout the programme lifecycle? Benefits must be constantly monitored to ensure that:
- Costs do not get any higher than anticipated
- The assumptions are accurate and up to date
- The solution or service will deliver enhanced, reduced or new Benefits.

Benefits are monitored through the use of Benefits management tools. Templates for these tools are available in the online Knowledge Centre.

The Benefits inventory

Identified Benefits are captured in a Benefits inventory. It is the first opportunity to detail the business Benefits to be potentially delivered by the programme in a single spreadsheet.

The purpose of the completed Benefits inventory is to give the Senior Responsible Owner, the Benefits Realisation Board and the Programme Team a greater understanding of the value and magnitude of the potential overall business Benefits.

A measurement should be suggested for each Benefit with a potential value. This can be based either on baseline data or on results from other organisations.

Benefit Cards

Benefits are then fully profiled on individual Benefit Cards, which are supported by a Benefits Realisation Plan. This is essential documentation, as it provides the basis for tracking and for ultimately assessing whether a Benefit has been achieved.

The Benefit Card defines the potential and expected level of Benefit to be achieved and a percentage calculation of the confidence that the Benefit will be realised. This figure is updated when Benefits are reviewed.

The Benefit Card is the primary means by which the Benefit is managed. Each Card is assigned an Owner, who must prove commitment to the delivery of the Benefit by signing the Card.

Because the Card must be signed by an Owner, it should contain sufficient detail to show how the Benefit has come to be and what it will achieve in quantifiable terms. In particular, the Card must contain:
- A clear description
- An owner
- A description of the type of Benefit (for example, to distinguish financial, non-financial: cashable or non-cashable)
- A target value

- A calculation mechanism including baseline data
- A list of assumptions
- Confidence rating
- Potential barriers to Benefits delivery.

Benefit Card			
Programme / Work stream			
Business Area / Process			
Benefit Owner			
Benefit Type			

Benefit Description		Total Benefit	Value
		Low	
		High	

Benefit Delivery Assumptions	High Target Assumptions

Benefit Measure & Baseline Data Source	Benefit Measure	Value	Unit of Measure
	Low		
	High		

Benefit Measure & Baseline Data Source	Benefit Measure	Value	Unit of Measure
	Low		
	High		

Barriers to Benefit Delivery

Barrier	Action to Remove Barrier to Benefit Delivery	Owner	Target Completion Date	Actual Completion Date	Sign off by Owner

Other Dependencies	Dependency Assumptions

Timing	Start	Full Benefit by	End

	% Confidence	Date	Name / Role	Signature
Identified				
Validated				
Enabled				
Realised				

Figure III.4.3 – Example Benefit Card

The Benefit Card should be maintained throughout the life of the Benefit. The status of the Benefit on the Benefit Card will change from Identified, to Validated, to Enabled and finally to Realised.

A confidence rating is included on the Benefit Card. This is established at, for example, 50% when the Benefit is Identified and, assuming the change goes to plan, should move to a higher confidence level at each review as the programme moves towards Benefits realisation.

More information about roles and responsibilities in Benefits management is included in Chapter 2 – CHAMPS2 governance.

FINAL WORDS

Benefits are not just the responsibility of programme managers or the Benefits Realisation Board. Everyone has a significant part to play in making Benefits happen. Transformation will change the way in which people work in many different ways. You may see some immediate Benefits but you are also contributing to much greater Benefits when viewed from the customer's or the organisation's perspective.

To illustrate this, here are some quotations about Benefits from delivered transformation programmes:

'The most important thing about the solution is that it delivers the Benefits. People come up with great design ideas but they're not always essential or relevant to the Benefits. If you're leading or supporting a transformation programme, you have to be tough. If it's only 'nice to have' and doesn't deliver any Benefits, then it's out.'

'Deliver early Benefits where possible. We were able to deliver a saving in the first eight months that essentially provided the budget to fund the rest of the transformation.'

'Involve the Benefit Owner from day one. They should have the full picture and a detailed understanding of the service or solution being proposed before they sign up to a Benefit Card.'

'As you scale up the programme for Design, new people will need to be brought up-to-speed with the Benefits. Develop a briefing process to help everyone understand how their work links together to deliver the Benefits.'

'Regular monitoring of the anticipated Benefits enables you to re-scope projects where they are not on target to achieve Benefits.'

'Benefits management is not about form-filling – it's a mindset that drives Benefits accountability and delivery.'

Section IV
Appendices

SECTION IV – APPENDICES

Appendix 1 – Core products

Essential documents within CHAMPS2 are called 'core products'. There are three types of core products:

- **Quality management products** help to assure quality and adherence to CHAMPS2, and provide exit criteria at the end of each phase.
- **Milestone products** are those which, when approved, allow the programme to continue to the next stage or phase. They provide control over the transformation journey.
- **Transformation products** support the evolution of the new processes, organisation and technology, and their successful delivery.

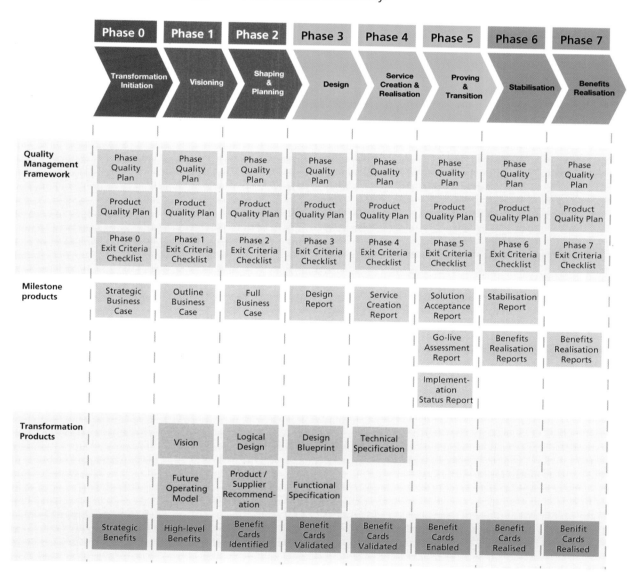

Figure IV.1 – Core products

QUALITY MANAGEMENT PRODUCTS

Product title	Phase Quality Plan
Purpose	To assure quality and tailor CHAMPS2 to programme needs
Description	The Phase Quality Plan allows Programme Teams to define which activities will be performed during the phase, what approach will be taken for each and which products will be delivered as part of that approach. The approach taken must satisfy the Exit Criteria Checklist used at the end of the phase
Composition	A list of stages and activities within the phase containing: ■ Suggested approach ■ Suggested products ■ Indicator whether activity selected or removed ■ Alternative approach ■ Alternative products
Input from	Phase Quality Plan template, Phase Exit Criteria Checklist
Used as an input to	Product Quality Plan, programme and project plans
Approved by	Senior Responsible Owner, Quality Assurance Function, Programme Manager (phases 3 to 6)

Product title	Product Quality Plan
Purpose	To assure the quality of products
Description	The Product Quality Plan defines the acceptance criteria and review /approval path for products identified within Phase Quality Plan
Composition	A list of products delivered within the phase containing: ■ Product description ■ Acceptance criteria ■ Persons accountable and responsible for product delivery ■ Reviewers of the product ■ Person accountable for approving the product
Input from	Phase Quality Plan, Product Quality Plan template
Used as an input to	Product breakdown structure, project plans
Approved by	Senior Responsible Owner, Quality Assurance Function, Programme Manager (phases 3 to 6)

Product title	Solution Acceptance Report		Phase 5
Purpose	To assess whether the solution is fit for purpose in the business		
Description	This report is based on the results of User Acceptance Testing and Operational Acceptance Testing. Testing should have proved that the solution works in real business situations and that the support processes work as well		
Composition	■ Overall status of the solution ■ List of components and their status ■ Summary of user acceptance testing results ■ Summary of operational acceptance testing results ■ Outstanding issues and actions		
Input from	Results of UAT and OAT		
Used as an input to	Go-live Assessment Report		
Approved by	Programme Board		

Product title	Go-live Assessment Report		Phase 5
Purpose	To assess readiness to implement the solution		
Description	This assessment is based on Go-live criteria and checks whether the solution can go live. It covers the resolution of any issues from UAT and OAT, completion of transitional tasks, and business area readiness for implementation		
Composition	■ Go-live criteria ■ Implementation readiness assessment ■ Outstanding issues and actions		
Input from	Go-live criteria		
Used as an input to	Go-live decision		
Approved by	Programme Board		

Product title	Implementation Status Report		Phase 5
Purpose	To assess the success of implementation		
Description	The status immediately after implementation needs to be reviewed to assess the success of implementation activities, the availability of all the components of the solution and any outstanding issues		
Composition	■ Activities completed against implementation plan ■ Status of components ■ Status of business areas ■ Outstanding issues and actions		
Input from	Implementation plan		
Used as an input to	Decommissioning or back-out decisions		
Approved by	Programme Board		

Product title	Stabilisation Report		Phase 6
Purpose	To mark the end of the stabilisation period for the solution		
Description	An assessment of readiness to hand over the support of the solution from the Programme Team to the business as usual support team		

Composition	■ Stabilisation criteria
	■ Stabilisation status
	  □ Processes
	  □ Organisation
	  □ Technology
	■ Readiness to hand over business support		

Input from	Stabilisation criteria		
Used as an input to	Decision to hand over support to the business as usual support team		
Approved by	Programme Board		

Product title	Benefits Realisation Report		Phase 6/7
Purpose	To assess achievements of anticipated Benefits		
Description	Benefits will be measured in predefined periods of time, as defined within the Benefits Realisation Plan. The findings will be documented within the Benefits Realisation Report, with suggested actions to address any under-achievement of Benefits		
Composition	■ Benefits measured this period and their expected and actual value ■ Reasons for under or over-achievement of Benefits ■ Actions to address under-achievement ■ Next Benefits realisation activities		
Input from	Benefit Card, Benefits Realisation Plan		
Used as an input to	Call Benefits Star Chamber		
Sent to	Benefits Realisation Board, Executive (information only)		

TRANSFORMATION PRODUCTS

Product title	Vision		Phase 1
Purpose	To set the target for transformational change		
Description	The Vision is an externally facing image of the future, describing what the change will achieve. It consists of an overarching Vision statement and a set of concrete Outcomes for different customer groups, employees or financial results		
Composition	■ Vision statement ■ Outcomes		
Input from	Strategic Business Case		
Used as an input to	Future Operating Model, Outline Business Case, Full Business Case		
Approved by	Executive (as part of OBC)		

Product title	Future Operating Model (FOM)		Phase 1
Purpose	To set the principles of the future operation		
Description	An internally facing image of the future, describing what the organisation will look like and how it will operate in order to achieve the Vision and desired Outcomes. This is the highest level of solution design, identifying key functions and key flows		

Composition	■ Principles of future operation
	■ A diagram showing key capabilities and relationships
	■ Aspects of future operation:
	  □ Processes
	  □ Organisation
	  □ Technology
	  □ Performance management
	■ How the Future Operation Model supports the Vision and Outcomes
	■ Requirements arising from the Future Operation Model		

Input from	Strategic Benefits		
Used as an input to	Logical Design		
Approved by	Process Design Authority, Organisation Design Authority, Technology Architecture Authority, Programme Board		

Product title	Benefit Card		Phase 2
Purpose	To define an individual Benefit and track its status		
Description	A separate Benefit Card is created for each Benefit and a Benefit Owner is assigned, who is responsible for realising the Benefit. The Benefit lifecycle is tracked on the card, consisting of four states: ■ Identified ■ Validated ■ Enabled ■ Realised		

Composition	■ Benefit description
	■ Benefit type
	■ Value
	■ Benefit measures
	■ Baseline source
	■ Assumptions
	■ Dependencies
	■ Barriers to Benefits delivery
	■ Timings for Benefit realisation
	■ Benefit status: Identified, Validated, Enabled, Realised
	■ For each Benefit status:
	  □ Confidence in achieving the Benefit expressed as a percentage
	  □ Date
	  □ Benefit Owner and signature		

Input from	Strategic Business Case, Outline Business Case		
Used as an input to	Full Business Case, Benefits Realisation Plan		
Approved by	Benefits Realisation Board, Benefit Owners		

Product title	Benefits Realisation Plan		Phase 2
Purpose	To provide a timeline for Benefits realisation		
Description	A document showing timescales for different groups of Benefits and outlining the activities required to measure them		
Composition	■ Benefits list and expected values ■ Benefits realisation milestones ■ Activities required to measure Benefits		
Input from	Benefit Cards, programme plan		
Used as an input to	Full Business Case, Benefits Realisation Report		
Approved by	Benefits Realisation Board, Executive gate		

Product title	Logical Design		Phase 2
Purpose	To provide a conceptual design of services and underlying processes		
Description	The document will identify key processes resulting from process decomposition and high-level organisation and technology design		
Composition	■ Service/Product design ■ Process decomposition ■ Organisation structure ■ Technology design ■ Identification of policies and standards to control the new processes ■ Requirements arising from the Logical Design		
Input from	Future Operating Model		
Used as an input to	Detailed design, Full Business Case		
Approved by	Process Design Authority, Organisation Design Authority, Technology Architecture Authority, Programme Board		

Product title	Product and Supplier Recommendation		Phase 2
Purpose	To select external products or service providers		
Description	The document presents the findings of the product and supplier evaluation and makes recommendations based on predefined selection criteria		
Composition	■ Business requirements ■ Shortlisted products and suppliers ■ Evaluation criteria ■ Evaluation results ■ Financial assessment ■ Recommendation		
Input from	Future Operating Model, Logical Design		
Used as an input to	Detailed design, Full Business Case		
Approved by	Programme Board		

Product title	Design Blueprint		Phase 3
Purpose	To document the detailed design to be used for the development of the solution		
Description	A document or set of documents describing in detail processes, organisation structure and technology and how all the components fit together		
Composition	■ Detailed process design, including process flow, roles involved, and the use of technology within the process ■ Organisation design, including organisation structure, roles descriptions and job profiles ■ Technology design – identification of all components that need to be installed or developed and how they fit together ■ Information flow and data design ■ Policies, standards and procedures that need to be developed ■ Requirements for the development of the solution		
Input from	Future Operating Model, Logical Design		
Used as an input to	Functional Specifications, system test plans, integration test plans		
Approved by	Process Design Authority, Organisation Design Authority, Technology Architecture Authority		

Product title	Functional Specification		Phase 3
Purpose	To describe how the component works from the user's perspective		
Description	The Functional Specification describes how the component works rather than how it is built. Each end-user technology component listed in the Design Blueprint, for example, on-line forms and reports, will be defined to the next level of detail in order to agree its functionality and operation within the relevant business area		
Composition	■ Purpose of the component and audience ■ Context ■ User operation ■ Look and feel ■ Data displayed/input		
Input from	Design Blueprint		
Used as an input to	Technical Specifications, unit test plans		
Approved by	Business managers		

Product title	Technical Specification	Phase 4
Purpose	To describe how the component is built	
Description	The Technical Specification describes the internal structure of component and the processing logic	
Composition	■ Functionality it needs to provide ■ Technical context ■ Internal design – composite parts and internal flows ■ Source and destination of data ■ Interfaces to other components	
Input from	Design Blueprint, Functional Specification	
Used as an input to	Development, unit test plans	
Approved by	Technology specialists	

Appendix 2 – Phase Exit Criteria Checklists

Phase Exit Criteria Checklists assess that all the activities, products and objectives have been delivered and the outcomes of the phase achieved.

Phase 0 Exit Criteria Checklist

Leadership commitment
- Are leaders fully engaged in transformation initiation?
- Is there sufficient buy-in for transformational change?
- Are leaders in agreement on the desired outcomes and priorities?
- Do leaders understand the potential scale of change and change impact?
- Has the change management approach been agreed with leaders?

Strategic need
- Is there a clear understanding of current business issues and performance?
- Have the key drivers for change been identified?
- Have customer needs and expectations been identified?
- Has the corporate strategy been reviewed?
- Are there any existing change programmes/projects already addressing some of these needs?

Strategic Outcomes
- Is there a high-level understanding of where the business wants to be in the future?
- Is the performance gap clearly understood?
- Have the priority areas for change been agreed?
- Have the ambitions for different aspects of the business been agreed?
- Have capability gaps been identified?

Strategic Business Case
- Are the business areas that may be included in the transformational change defined?
- Is there a clear understanding of the transformation start and end points, i.e. strategic need and strategic Outcomes?
- Is the difference the potential transformation will make clearly articulated (strategic Benefits)?
- Does it provide a high-level justification for transformation, i.e. strategic Benefits against indicative cost?

Phase 1 Exit Criteria Checklist

Vision
- Is there a Vision statement for the business area?
- Are Outcomes for different customer groups clearly defined?
- Do they represent the needs of the respective customer groups?
- Have any Outcomes for employees been identified?
- Have any financial Outcomes been defined?
- Are the Outcomes measurable?
- Is there sufficient buy-in from senior stakeholders for this Vision?

Future Operating Model
- Is there a Future Operating Model for the business area?
- Does the Future Operating Model reflect the Vision and desired Outcomes?
- Do key stakeholders fully understand the principles of the future operation of the business area?
- Is there a high-level understanding of future processes, organisation structure and technology?
- Is there a high-level understanding of capability gaps?
- Have any priorities for change within the Future Operating Model been identified?
- Have any overlaps with current change initiatives been identified?

Outline Business Case
- Does the Outline Business Case clearly describe the future for the business?
- Has the scope of potential transformational change been determined?
- Does it comply with relevant corporate strategies, policies and legislation?
- Have the high-level Benefits been defined and do they support the strategic Benefits?
- Have indicative costs and timescales been determined?
- Have any potential risks been considered?
- Are the scale of this change and the change impact understood?
- Have stakeholders, including customers, been consulted on the direction described in the Outline Business Case?
- Is there a commitment from senior stakeholders to this direction?

Phase 2 Exit Criteria Checklist

Logical Design

- Is there a clear understanding of services or products that will be offered by the business in the future?
    - ☐ Processes: Have the high-level processes and sub-processes been identified and are they integrated?
    - ☐ Organisation: Is there a high-level organisation structure with clear accountabilities and responsibilities for each team?
    - ☐ Technology: Has the high-level technology been identified?
- Does the new design support the desired Outcomes and Benefits?
- Does the new design comply with relevant corporate strategies, policies and legislation?
- Is the change impact of the new design fully understood?
- Have stakeholders, including customers, been consulted on the key elements of Logical Design?
- Is there a sufficient buy-in from senior stakeholders for this design?

Product and supplier selection

- Have the business requirements been clearly formulated?
- Did the product and supplier selection process follow the company's standards?
- Do the selected products fit into Logical Design?
- Do the selected products support the desired Outcomes and Benefits?

Benefits

- Is there a comprehensive inventory of Benefits to be delivered by the programme?
- Have all three categories of Benefits been explored, namely: customers, employees and efficiencies?
- Are all Benefits measurable, with realistic values?
- Have any assumptions or potential barriers been identified?
- Has each Benefit been documented on a Benefit Card?
- Do Benefit Owners fully understand the link between the changes within their area and the Benefits?
- Are all Benefits in the status 'Identified' and signed by the Benefit Owner?
- Is there a Benefits Realisation Plan in place?

Programme planning

- Is there a clear understanding of the capability gap and the work that will need to be undertaken?
- Has the programme structure been defined?
- Is there a definite list of projects that form a project portfolio?
- Are high-level plans available for programme delivery?
- Have any dependencies or overlaps with other change initiatives been resolved?
- Is a detailed resource plan in place?
- Have the programme costs been determined?

Programme Governance

- Has the programme organisation structure been agreed?
- Have the roles and responsibilities been defined?
- Are the key strategies in place?

Full Business Case

- Is there a Full Business Case that justifies the transformation programme?
- Are the scope and objectives of the programme clearly defined?
- Are the risks clearly understood?
- Are the cost and time implications understood?
- Does it provide a clear evaluation of Benefits versus costs?
- Has funding been secured via the Full Business Case?
- Is the impact of change understood?
- Have stakeholders, including customers, been consulted on the direction described in the Full Business Case?
- Is there sufficient commitment from senior stakeholders to the proposed change programme?

Phase 3 Exit Criteria Checklist

Detailed design
- Processes:
  - ☐ Are there detailed process maps available for the new processes?
  - ☐ Do they clearly communicate which roles perform the processes and where the technology is used?
  - ☐ Is there sufficient integration between processes?
- Organisation:
  - ☐ Have the jobs within the new organisation structure been defined?
  - ☐ Have the high-level training needs been identified?
- Technology:
  - ☐ Have the application, data and technology architecture been agreed?
  - ☐ Has the state of the current data been assessed?
  - ☐ Is there a data migration strategy in place?
- Does the detailed design support the desired Outcomes and Benefits?
- Does the detailed design comply with relevant corporate strategies, policies and legislation?
- Have interested parties, including customers, been consulted on the relevant parts of the design?

Design Blueprint
- Is there a clear view of how processes, organisation structure and technology fit together?
- Is a sufficient level of detail available to enable service creation?
- Is a full list of components that need to be created, amended or purchased available?
  - ☐ Processes: policies, standards and procedures
  - ☐ Organisation: jobs, roles, training courses
  - ☐ Technology: applications, interfaces etc.

Benefits
- Have all the Benefits been Validated?
- Are all Benefit Cards Validated and signed by Benefit Owners?
- Does the Benefits Realisation Plan reflect any changes to Benefits?
- Has the Full Business Case been revised and approved?
- Is there continuing commitment from senior stakeholders to this change programme?

Design Report
- Do senior stakeholders understand the key elements of detailed design?
- Are any changes to Benefits fully understood?
- Is the change impact of the new solution fully understood?
- Are the senior stakeholders clear on the work that will now need to be undertaken by the Programme Team?

Functional Specifications
- Have all the Functional Specifications been completed and reviewed by the business?
- Do they clearly communicate how the components will work from a user perspective?

Phase 4 Exit Criteria Checklist

Creation
- Have technical specifications been produced for relevant components?
- Has a detailed training needs analysis been completed?
- Have all the components been created, amended, purchased or configured?
  - ☐ Processes: policies, standards, procedures, service level agreements
  - ☐ Organisation: job descriptions, person specifications, training courses
  - ☐ Technology: hardware, software, applications, interfaces, reports, forms, etc.
- Is all the documentation fully up to date, including any changes to design documents and Functional Specifications?

Testing
- Have the processes and organisation structure been through a business scenario walkthrough?
- Has all unit testing been completed and do the individual components work to the Functional and Technical Specifications?
- Has all system testing been completed and do the systems work to the Functional Specifications and Design Blueprint?
- Has all integration testing been completed and do the end-to-end processes work to the Design Blueprint and Logical Design?
- Is there a clear understanding of any outstanding issues?

Data
- Has data cleansing started?
- Has the trial data migration run been completed?
- Has the collection of baseline data for Benefits realisation started?

Benefits
- Were all the Benefits Validated once the solution was completed?
- Are all Benefit Cards Validated and signed by Benefit Owners?
- Does the Benefits Realisation Plan reflect any changes to Benefits?

Service Creation Report
- Are any changes to Benefits fully understood?
- Is the change impact of the new solution fully understood?
- Are senior stakeholders confident about the completeness of the solution?
- Are senior stakeholders satisfied with the level of testing undertaken?
- Are senior stakeholders aware of any outstanding issues and actions?

Phase 5 Exit Criteria Checklist

Acceptance testing
- Has all User Acceptance Testing (UAT) been completed and do the end-to-end processes meet the business requirements?
- Has all Operational Acceptance Testing (OAT) been completed and does the solution meet support requirements?
- Is there a clear understanding of any outstanding issues?
- Has the solution been accepted by the business?

Transition
- Processes:
  - ☐ Have any changes to processes or related documentation been prepared, e.g. procedures?
- Organisation:
  - ☐ Have all job changes been completed and all jobs populated?
  - ☐ Has training been completed to the required level?
  - ☐ Have work spaces been prepared for change?
- Technology:
  - ☐ Have relevant technology components been deployed in advance?
  - ☐ Has data cleansing been completed?
  - ☐ Has trial data migration been completed?
- Have Benefits baseline data been collected before implementation?
- Have employees received clear communications about the changes that affect them?

Implementation
- Have the Go-live criteria been defined and have these been met?
- Was there sufficient planning for implementation, including:
  - ☐ Implementation plans
  - ☐ Business Continuity plans
  - ☐ Back out plans?
- Have all the implementation tasks been completed?
- Does the Implementation Status Report effectively communicate the implementation status of different components and individual business areas?
- Are any implementation issues understood and actions agreed?
- Were appropriate communications issued prior to, and after, implementation?

Benefits
- Have all Benefits been Enabled?
- If the implementation has not been fully completed, is the impact on Benefits clear?
- For enabled Benefits, have the Benefit Cards been set to status Enabled and signed by Benefit Owners?
- Does the Benefits Realisation Plan reflect any changes to Benefits?

Phase 6 Exit Criteria Checklist

Benefits realisation
- Have the early Benefits been successfully measured?
- For any Benefits that have been achieved, have the Benefit Cards been set to status 'Realised' and signed by the Benefit Owner?
- Is the appropriate level of achievement of Benefits recorded in the Benefits Realisation Report?
- Are the reasons for any underachievement of Benefits understood and actions agreed?
- Has the Benefits Realisation Plan been amended accordingly?
- Are senior stakeholders fully aware of the status of Benefits realisation?

Stabilisation
- Processes: Have any changes to processes or related documentation, e.g. procedures, been completed?
- Organisation: Have all job changes and additional training been completed?
- Technology: Is the technology stable and reaching required performance levels?
- Are the support processes stable?
- Were there stabilisation criteria defined and have these been met?

Programme closedown
- Has the evaluation of the transformation journey been completed?
- Have the lessons learnt been consolidated?
- Has the business support been handed over to the business as usual (BAU) support team?
- Has the final handover of documentation to the business been completed?
- Are the Benefits fully owned by the business now?
- Has a Benefits Realisation Plan Owner been appointed?
- Has the programme closedown checklist been completed and the programme closed down?

Phase 7 Exit Criteria Checklist

Benefits realisation
- Have all the Benefits been realised according to the Benefits Realisation Plan?
- Have Benefits Cards been set to the status Realised and signed by the Benefit Owner?
- Has the Benefits Realisation Report effectively communicated the achievement of Benefits?
- Have senior stakeholders been informed of the end of Benefits realisation?

Continuous improvement
- Are any further improvements to the transformed business being assessed against the Vision, desired Outcomes and Benefits?
- Have all the actions arising from Benefits realisation been completed?
- Are continuous improvement activities seeking opportunities to add new Benefits?

Appendix 3 – Glossary

A

Ability A quality that permits or facilitates achievement or accomplishment.

Accountable Accepting responsibility and being answerable for actions.

Activity 1. CHAMPS2: a phase consisting of stages that, in turn, consist of activities
2. PRINCE2: the smallest self-contained unit of work used in project planning.

Affordable Statement of available funding and estimates of projected whole-life cost of programme or project.

Approval A formal acceptance of a product, often confirmed by a signature.

As-is Current state of the business, before transformational change has occurred. A transformational change programme will move the business from its 'as-is' state to its 'to-be'.

B

Back-out plan A plan to return to the original state in case the implementation of a new business process or supporting system fails.

Baseline A snapshot of the state of inputs/outputs frozen at a point in time for a particular process. A baseline should be recorded to establish a starting point to measure the changes achieved with any business change improvement.

Benefit Benefits are the measurable difference we will make for the business and its customers through transformation.

Cashable Delivering the same for less money: financial Benefits that actually release money and result in a physical change to a business area's budget. An example of this would be processing the same number of applications at a lower cost.

Enabled A status of Benefit at the end of phase 5 – Proving and Transition, when the solution has been moved to live operation.

Financial A Benefit with a financial advantage, such as an efficiency saving.

Identified A status of Benefit at the end of phase 2 – Shaping and Planning. At this point a Benefit value and a Benefit Owner will have been assigned and a Benefit Card will have been approved and signed by the Benefit Owner, detailing the anticipated business Benefits.

Intangible Benefits that are hard to measure (such as more accurate information, increased awareness).

Non-cashable Financial Benefits that will result in an increase of volume or quality in the business for the same money. An example of this would be processing an increased number of applications for the same cost.

Non-financial Benefits which do not have a direct impact on costs or revenue, for example, customer satisfaction, reputation.

Realised A status when measurable improvement has been achieved, for example, financial savings or customer satisfaction.

Tangible Benefits that can be measured (such as financial savings or reduced processing time).

Validated A status of Benefit at the end of phase 3 – Design, when the Benefit value is recalculated based on a better understanding of what the solution will deliver.

Benefit Owner A person from the business who is accountable for ensuring that business Benefits are realised. In the case of financial Benefits it will be a budget holder from the area responsible for releasing the cash.

Benefit Card A document created for each business Benefit, which details the status, value and type of business Benefit that will be provided by a transformation programme. Each Benefit Card is approved and signed by a Benefit Owner from the business and is used for tracking the status of the Benefit throughout its lifecycle.

Benefits Coordinator A coordinating role used where there are multiple transformational change programmes. This role coordinates the delivery of all Benefits, ensures that no double counting of Benefits takes place and monitors Benefits delivery against the Benefits Realisation Plan.

Benefits inventory A spreadsheet listing the potential Benefits that will be delivered by the transformational change programme. It forms the basis for the creation of Benefit Cards.

Benefits realisation Measuring Benefits and proving that they have been achieved.

Benefits Realisation Board A group overseeing Benefits across the organisation, ensuring that the aims are realistic and the potential gain from Benefits is maximised.

Benefits Realisation Plan A document showing timescales for different groups of Benefits and outlining the activities required to measure them.

Benefits Realisation Plan Owner Takes responsibility for the ongoing management and delivery of Benefits.

Benefits Realisation Report Benefits will be measured in predefined periods of time, as defined within the Benefits Realisation Plan. The findings will be documented within the Benefits Realisation Report, with suggested actions to address any under-achievement of Benefits.

Benefits Star Chamber A group of senior executives meeting on an ad hoc basis to resolve Benefits realisation issues and bring together interested parties to remove barriers to Benefits realisation.

Blueprint Design Blueprint – a document produced at the end of detailed design containing detailed design of processes, organisation, supporting technology, information and data.

Budget Quantification of resources needed to achieve a task by a set time, within which the task owners are required to work. A budget consists of a financial and/or quantitative statement, prepared and approved prior to a defined period.

Budget holder A person with financial responsibility and the budget for the business area.

Business area A term used to define the area(s) of the organisation that will be involved in a transformation programme. Business area for transformation does not necessarily relate to a specific section or department within the current organisation structure.

Business area imperatives The priority areas ('must haves') within the business area.

Business area readiness The state of preparation for implementation, in terms of organisation structure, training, data preparation, support arrangements and so on.

Business Change Manager A person from the business who would prepare the business area for the change (for example, ensuring processes have been accepted and training is in place, assisting with data migration and so on).

Business continuity plan Documented arrangements and procedures that enable the business area to continue to provide the service to customers during the change or other interruptions.

Business requirements Requirements reflecting the needs of the business, defined during design and to be used to procure or develop the solution.

Business scenario A particular path through the business area's processes simulating a real- life situation.

C

Capability The capability of a product, process, a person or organisation is the ability to perform a specific function.

Capability gap The difference between the current business capabilities within a business area and the future required business capabilities defined by the transformation.

Capability matrix Tool used to define the level of current capabilities within the organisation, by business area, and to compare these with the future capabilities needed. This defines the 'capability gap'.

Change driver A reason for change, either internal or external (for example, customer expectations, legislation).

Change impact Effect of transformation on organisation structure, people, systems, data, ways of working and so on.

Change imperatives The key reasons and drivers for any transformational change. The most important aspects of the business that must be changed.

Change management Handling people-related aspects and impacts of transformational change such as defining job roles, communications and managing the transition from the existing organisation to the new organisation.

Change request A request needed to obtain formal approval for changes to the scope, design, methods, costs or planned aspects of a project. Change requests may arise through changes in the business or issues in the project.

Communication plan A document describing how the stakeholders and interested parties will be kept informed during the programme or project.

Continuous improvement Incremental improvement of existing processes, as opposed to step improvement brought by transformational change.

Core products Essential documents within CHAMPS2. There are three types: milestone products, transformation products and quality management products. See appendix 1 for a full list.

Cost Benefit case Comparison of Benefits and the investment required to deliver the Benefits.

Cost A Programme/project cost: an overall cost of the programme/project derived from resource costs, material costs, with contingency applied.

Customer A person or an organisation that uses or is affected by organisation's products or services (such as citizens, small businesses, visitors).

Customer experience Customer perception of the services provided by the organisation, based on their own judgment criteria, rather than the organisation's internal performance indicators.

D

Data Facts, for example, numbers, text, images and sound, in a form that is suitable for storage in, or processing by, a computer.

Data cleansing Updating the data so that it can be converted successfully to the format required by the new system (such as putting numerical values into empty fields or standardising addresses).

Data enrichment Adding information that did not exist, but is required by the new data structures (for example, new classification).

Data migration The process of translating data from one format to another. Data migration is necessary when an organisation decides to use a new information technology system that is incompatible with the current system.

Defect management Recording, monitoring and resolving the problems encountered during testing.

Deliverable An item that the project has to deliver. Often, 'deliverable' represents a group of products delivered together.

Dependency Precedence relationship. Restriction that one activity has to precede, either in part or in total, another activity. Dependencies can be also defined between programmes and projects.

Design Blueprint A document that details the design of all the components that make up a solution and how they fit together.

Design Report The Design Report is a summary of the design, which is suitable for a business audience and is submitted to the Programme Board. It presents the outcomes of the Design Blueprint and explores how the completed design will affect the business.

Detailed design A design phase that builds on the processes identified within Logical Design and defines how the service will operate, including the flow of activities and information, who performs them and the tools and supporting systems involved.

E

Effectiveness Targeting processes on customer needs and achieving customer satisfaction. 'Doing the right things'.

Efficiency Performing process with fewer inputs or producing more outputs compared to a similar process, to achieve the objectives of the process. 'Doing things right'.

End-user The person or group who will use the deliverable(s) of the project.

Executive Typically senior leaders with a clear view of the strategic needs of the organisation and its customers. They will be involved in championing the programme for change and communicating the Outcomes to be achieved.

F

FBC See: Full Business Case

Floorwalker A person providing post implementation support directly in the business area before the new solution is fully embedded.

FOM See: Future Operating Model

Full Business Case (FBC) A document providing justification for investment in transformational change, based on Benefits, costs and risks. It is used to obtain management approval and commitment.

Functional Specification The Functional Specification describes how a component works from the user's perspective, rather than how it is built. Each end-user technology component listed in the Design Blueprint will be defined to the next level of detail in order to agree its functionality and operation within the relevant business area.

Future Operating Model (FOM) A very high-level design that sets out the composition and operation of the future organisation that will deliver the desired Outcomes and the Vision.

G

Gate A review of a programme/project carried out at key decision points by a team of experienced people, independent of the programme/project team.

Go-live The point at which the new processes, organisational roles and responsibilities and technology are put into operation.

Go-live Assessment Report Assessment of readiness to implement the solution based on Go-live criteria.

Go-live criteria Criteria that will be used to judge whether the implementation of the solution into live operation can go ahead.

Governance Programme governance consists of bodies (persons or committees) overseeing the programme delivery and key programme management strategies.

I

Impact assessment The assessment of the impact of proposed changes (such as process change, organisational change, technological change, behavioural change).

Implementation plan A detailed schedule of tasks and products to implement a solution.

Implementation Status Report Assessment of the success of implementation. The status immediately after implementation needs to be reviewed to assess the success of implementation activities, the availability of all the components of the solution, and any outstanding issues.

Information A collection of data organised in a way that adds to the knowledge of the person receiving it.

Interface A piece of hardware or software to enable two systems to communicate.

Issue A problem, query, concern or change that affects the programme and requires management intervention and action to resolve. Issues (as distinct from risks) are problems that already exist.

J

Job A collection of functions, tasks, duties, and responsibilities assigned to one or more positions which require work of the same nature and level. A job holder may undertake a number of roles.

Job profile The clustered roles documented on the role cards are put into logical groups that could be performed by one person and a job profile is created for each group.

K

Key performance indicators (KPI) Performance indicators by which the performance of the whole organisation is measured.

Knowledge Information that is used for understanding or doing something or which has an intent attached to it. Whereas information can be placed onto a computer, knowledge exists in the people's heads.

Knowledge Centre Online CHAMPS2 resource which includes diagrams and activity descriptions, templates, examples and 'how to' documents, and which can be found at www.champs2.info.

Knowledge transfer Passing the knowledge from Programme Teams to the business area prior to implementation.

KPI See: Key performance indicators

L

Lessons learnt Learning points from the programme that could be usefully applied to other change programmes. Within CHAMPS2 lessons learnt will be collected at the end of each phase.

Logical Design A conceptual design that will define what processes, organisation structure and technology components will make up the service. This requires the decomposition of processes into sub-processes and the identification of inputs, outputs and controls (or policies) that govern each process.

M

Measures of success Defining what constitutes success, what 'good' looks like.

Milestone A key event on the project plan. Milestones are used to monitor progress at summary level.

Milestone products Control documents which, when approved, allow the programme to continue to the next stage or phase. Appendix 1 includes a full list of milestone products.

MSP Managing Successful Programmes, a structured framework for programme management.

Must-dos The most important processes or activities that must be included in the future operation.

Must-haves The most important business areas or business policies that must be included in the future operation.

O

OAT See: Testing -> Operational acceptance testing

OBC See: Outline Business Case.

Objective Pre-determined results towards which effort is directed.

Organisation Design Authority Role which oversees and approves organisation design such as roles, team composition and leadership.

Organisation structure The way in which an organisation has arranged its lines of authority and communication, and allocated duties and responsibilities.

Outcome The result of change, normally affecting real-world behaviours or circumstances (MSP definition). For example, application processing will take three days; customer satisfaction will be 70%.

Outline Business Case (OBC) Communicates clearly the direction for the transformational change, before any detailed design and planning take place. It should provide a compelling argument for pursuing the future outlined in the Vision, Outcomes and Future Operating Model and justify the development of a Full Business Case. It also outlines the Benefits and indicative costs of the transformation.

Output Components, for example IT systems, procedures, job descriptions, that enable Outcomes.

P

Performance A measure of an organisation's progress towards its goals.

Performance indicators (PI) Quantifiable measurements, agreed beforehand, that reflect the critical success factors of an organisation, individual function or a process.

Phase A part of the transformational change journey. CHAMPS2 consists of eight phases.

Phase Exit Criteria Checklist A checklist to assess that all the outcomes have been achieved and delivered, based on the evidence provided .

Phase Quality Plan A document that defines which activities will be performed by the programme during a particular phase, what approach will be taken for each activity, and

which products will be delivered.

PMO See: Programme management office

Policy A set of principles that guide the decisions within a particular business area.

PRINCE2 A structured project management method containing a series of processes which cover all the activities needed on a project from starting up to closing down.

Procedure A set of instructions that guide the execution of a particular process.

Process A sequence of activities that must be performed to bring about a particular Outcome, in terms of information to be gathered, decisions to be made and results that must be achieved.

Process decomposition Breaking down a high-level process into sub-processes.

Process Design Authority Someone who oversees the design of related processes. They will have expertise in the business area and make sure the processes fit together.

Product Any input to, or output from, a project. PRINCE2 distinguishes between management products, which are produced as part of the management or quality processes, and specialist products, which make up the final deliverable. CHAMPS2 highlights core products which document the development of the solution and control progress.

Product and Supplier Recommendation Presents the findings of the product and supplier evaluation and makes recommendations based on predefined selection criteria.

Product Quality Plan Defines each product to be produced by the programme during a particular phase detailing who is responsible and accountable for delivery, acceptance criteria, reviews and approval.

Programme A portfolio of projects selected, planned and managed in a co-ordinated way.

Programme Board A body that provides leadership and direction for the programme, releases investment and approves progress through the gates.

Programme costing Deriving programme costs from estimates of activities and costs of resources.

Programme Director An optional role to take over some of the Senior Responsible Owner's responsibilities related to directing the programme.

Programme lifecycle Programme phases

from Shaping and Planning to Stabilisation, represented by CHAMPS2 phases 2 to 6.

Programme management office (PMO) A group set up to provide administrative services to the programme.

Programme Manager Individual responsible for programme delivery and managing risks, issues and dependencies between projects in a portfolio.

Programme plan A plan containing all projects within the program with key milestones.

Programme structure A structure of projects and work streams that form a programme.

Programme Team A team consisting of project teams and cross project roles that will deliver the Outcomes required by the programme.

Project Unique set of co-ordinated activities, with definite starting and finishing points, undertaken by an individual or organisation to meet specific objectives within defined time, cost and performance parameters.

Project Manager A person responsible for project delivery, risks and issues.

Project portfolio The list of all the projects that together will deliver the required capability to achieve the programme Outcomes.

Q

Quality A trait or characteristic used to measure the degree of excellence of a product or service.

Quality Assurance The process of evaluating overall project performance on a regular basis to provide confidence that the project will satisfy the relevant quality standards.

Quality Management Framework Provides a quality structure and tools which bring consistency and which support the use of the CHAMPS2 method in the most effective and efficient way. See the Quality Management Framework chapter in section III.

Quality management products Quality management products are documents which are designed to help the Programme Team be clear about what they need to produce, to what standard and in what sequence. See the Quality Management Framework chapter in section III.

Quick fix A hastily contrived remedy that alleviates a problem only for the time being, or a fix that can be put in place relatively quickly as part of other work being completed.

Quick win Small steps or initiatives that will

produce immediate, positive results. 'Quick wins' may be generated as part of a much larger programme or project.

R

RAG Red, amber, green status for monitoring progress.

Recommendation Within procurement: a selection of solution and supplier submitted to the appropriate governance for approval.

Repository A central place where information is stored.

Requirements What needs to be included in the design or build of the solution to enable specific functionality or business rules.

Resource Any variable that is required for the completion of an activity and may constrain the project. Resources can be people, equipment, facilities, funding or anything else needed to perform the work of a project.

Responsibility Having a job or duty to do something.

Risk A negative threat or positive opportunity that might affect the course of the programme. The severity of the risk is determined from the probability of it occurring and the impact it would have.

Risk assessment The process of identifying potential risks and assessing the likelihood of their occurrence and the impact they would have.

Risk impact The extent of what would happen if the risk materialised.

Risk management A process of identifying, analysing, evaluating, treating and monitoring risks. The decisions are made to accept known risks or implement actions to reduce the consequences or probability of occurrence.

Risk mitigation Actions to be taken to reduce the impact or probability of the risk.

Role A set of responsibilities, activities and authorisations. A role may be undertaken by a number of different job-holders.

S

SBC See: Strategic Business Case

Scope The boundaries of what a programme or project will cover.

Senior Business Owner An optional role to take over some of the Senior Responsible Owner's responsibilities to provide leadership within business areas affected by the programme.

Senior Responsible Owner (SRO) MSP terminology: A person ultimately accountable for the success of the programme. A person representing business commitment to the programme and who ensures that the programme is appropriately funded.

Service creation Follows the design phase and includes the development, amendment or purchase of the designed solution and organisation.

Service Creation Report A report produced at the end of phase 4 indicating the status of the solution after unit testing, system testing and integration testing. It marks the completion of the solution by the Programme Team.

Service imperatives The most important services and business processes ('must do') within the business area.

Service level agreement (SLA) A contract where the level and standards of service and any responsibilities are formally agreed between two or more parties to make sure there is a common understanding.

Service provider An organisation or a team delivering a particular capability (for example, an online payments service provider, external storage provider).

Skill Ability, usually learned and acquired through training.

SMART Specific, Measurable, Achievable, Realistic and Time-limited. Used to describe Benefits and Outcomes.

Solution Acceptance Report Assessment by the business that the solution is fit for purpose. This report is based on the results of user acceptance testing and operational acceptance testing.

Specification 1. *Procurement:* presents prospective suppliers with a clear, accurate and full description of the organisation's needs, and so enables them to propose a solution to meet those needs. **2.** *Service creation:* detailed information needed to develop and test the components, done in two stages: the Functional Specification and the Technical Specification.

Sponsor Another name for the role of Senior Responsible Owner.

Stabilisation Report An assessment of readiness to hand over the support of the solution from the Programme Team to the business as usual support team.

Stage 1. CHAMPS2 Method: A phase consists of stages, which, in turn, consist of activities. **2.** PRINCE2: A natural high-level subsection of a project that has its own organisational structure, lifespan and manager.

Stakeholder Parties with an interest in the execution and Outcome of a programme/project. They would include both those that can affect the success or will be affected by the Outcomes of the programme/project.

Standard A set of measures that need to be achieved to comply with policy.

Strategic Business Case (SBC) A high-level business case which outlines the strategic need and strategic Outcomes and outlines Benefits and indicative costs.

Strategic Outcome High-level results sought by the organisation and expressed as the effect of change on customers, employees or efficiency.

Super user Members of a business area who have acquired an in-depth knowledge of the solution either through intensive training or participation in the programme.

Supplier The group or groups responsible for the supply of the project's specialist products.

Swimlane A process diagram that indicates which roles perform particular activities.

T

Technical cutover A point when the deployed technology is switched to live operation.

Technical Specification Describes the internal structure of the component and the processing logic.

Technology Architecture Authority Role which oversees and approves technology design of the solution.

Testing:

Integration testing End-to-end process testing by the Programme Team.

Operational acceptance testing (OAT) The purpose of Operational Acceptance Testing is to prove that the solution can be successfully supported once it goes live and will achieve expected performance levels.

Regression testing Regression testing helps to ensure that changes made to systems or introduction of new systems do not break other previously working parts of the systems.

Stress testing Checking whether the application can withstand an extreme volume of activities and data and finding out at what point the application fails or its performance degrades.

System testing Testing all processes within a particular application system (for example, a SAP module).

Unit testing Proving that individual units of built components work to detailed specifications.

User acceptance testing (UAT) End-to-end testing of processes by the business using the finished solution to verify that the solution is fit for implementation.

Test scenarios A test scenario describes a business situation that should be tested. It should include the preconditions (what relevant data exists at the start of the test case execution) and inputs.

Test schedule A sequence of test with dependencies, estimates on timing and resource allocation.

TNA See: Training needs analysis

Top-down approach An approach to organisation or planning that is built from high-level principles down to components.

Training needs analysis (TNA) Assessment of current skills within the business area against the competencies required in the future and identification of the training required.

Tranche Projects grouped by Benefits delivery, which would be followed by a common Benefits Realisation project.

Transformation products Transformational products are documents which support overall transformation, describe the solution and provide information to the Programme Board and the Programme Team. Appendix 1 has a full list of transformation products.

Transition The period leading up to the point where the business area will physically change from the old way of working to the new.

Transition plan A plan of activities required for the transition period to a new operation, verification of success of transition and a back-out plan.

U

UAT See: Testing -> User acceptance Testing

User The person or group who will use the outputs of a transformation programme or project. This can be a customer or an internal user.

V

Vision An image of the future which is expressed as a Vision statement and Outcomes.

Vision statement A broad, aspirational image of the future that an organisation is aiming to achieve.

W

Work stream A subdivision of the programme (programme work stream) or a project (project work stream).

Appendix 4 – Further Reading

Official CHAMPS2 site – www.champs2.info

Case study on Service Birmingham – www.capita.co.uk/about-us/Pages/
Birmingham.aspx

PRINCE2 – www.ogc.gov.uk/methods_prince_2.asp

MSP – www.ogc.gov.uk/guidance_managing_successful_
programmes_4442.asp

Business transformation in Birmingham – www.birmingham.gov.uk/btsp

Cabinet Office, Transformational Government (2005) –
www.cabinetoffice.gov.uk/media/141734/transgov-strategy.pdf

Performance and Innovation Unit (1999), *e-commerce@its.best.uk*,
Cabinet Office, UK

Burnes, B. (2000) *Managing Change: A strategic approach to
organisational dynamics*, Prentice Hall

Cameron, E. and Green, M. (2nd Ed 2009) *Making Sense of Change
Management: A complete guide to the models, tools and techniques of
organisational change*, Kogan Page

Clarke, T and Clegg, S (2000) *Changing Paradigms: The transformation
of management knowledge for the twenty-first century*, HarperCollins,
London

Daniel Hunt, V. (1996) *Process Mapping: How to re-engineer your business
processes*, John Wiley and Sons

Damelio, R. (1996) *The Basics of Process Mapping*, Productivity Press Inc

Feldman, C. G. (1998) *The Practical Guide to Business Process
Re-engineering using IDEF0*, Dorset House Publishing

Hammer, M., Champy, J. (1993) *Re-engineering the Corporation:
A manifesto for business revolution*, Harper Collins, London

Hendry, C. (1995) *Human Resource Management: A strategic approach
to employment*, Butterworth Heinemann

Joyce, P. (1999) *Strategic Management for the Public Services*, Open
University Press

Markus M. L. and Benjamin R. (1997) 'IT-Enabled Organizational Change: new developments for IT specialists', in Sauer C., Yetton PW and Associates, *Steps to the Future: Fresh thinking on the management of IT-based organizational transformation*, Jossey-Bass, San Francisco

OGC, (2009) *Managing Successful Projects with PRINCE2: 2009 Edition*, Stationery Office Books

Reiss, G. et al (2006) *The Gower Handbook of Programme Management*, Gower Publishing Ltd

Shark, A. R. and Toporkoff, S. (2010) *Beyond eGovernment – Measuring Performance: A Global Perspective*, Public Technology Institute (Evans, G. 'From e-Government to Transformation')

Sowden, R. and OGC (2007) *Managing Successful Programmes*, Stationery Office Books

Venning, C. and OGC (2007) *Managing portfolios of change with MSP for programmes and PRINCE2 for projects: Integrating MSP and PRINCE2*, Stationery Office Books

Williams, D and Parr, T. (2006) *Enterprise Programme Management: Delivering Value*, Palgrave Macmillan

Index